Transmuted 010

'Speak for Yourself'

A journal for gender non-normative artists,
writers, and creatives.

First published in December 2024

Edited, illustrated, and cover designed by Dorian Rose
Proofread by Anna Rose and Dorian Rose (not related!)

All profits go towards the continuation of the journal, projects,
and running costs of Transmuted.

A Cataloguing in Publication Data record for this book is available from the British Library
ISBN 978 1 917633 00 0

Copyright © 2024 Transmuted CIC and contributors
All Rights Reserved

Each author asserts their moral right to be identified as the owner of their
respective work in accordance with the Copyright, Designs and Patents Act 1998.

No part of this publication may be distributed for resale. This publication may be reproduced, stored in a retreval system, distributed, or transmitted in any form (including printing, photocopying, recording, and other methods) without the prior written permission of the copyright holders - with the requirement that attribution is given to the holders, in accordance with Creative Commons.

Printed in the United Kingdom.

Transmuted CIC is a community interest company registered England and Wales
(Company No. 15435240)

EDITORS' NOTE

Eyup folks!

We are so proud to have made it to ten issues of Transmuted (TransMuted, or however you write it - I dunno)! While I personally can see my editing skills slowly getting better over each issue, I still can't believe we've made it this far.

We have hit a couple bumps in the road along the way (perhaps an understatement), but in a time where many trans-oriented groups and projects have had to pack up and close shop due to the struggles of running such a difficult enterprise, we count each and every one of our blessings with the knowledge that - whatever happens - we have done our darndest to bring something positive to our communities.

I had the great opportunity of working writer-journalist jane fae and some folks from TransActual on her book *Transitions: the UnheardStories* - which you can get from TransActual's website (it is a great resource for cis people). This experience made me much less anxious about the pertinent question, 'how do people design and print PUR bound books?', and has joyfully resulted in this publication featuring - for the first time in Transmuted's history - both PUR binding and an ISBN! We are hoping to publish books in the future alongside our other escapades, using what we've learned to build a trans-only, trans-friendly (you would hope they go hand-in-hand) publisher - so if you've got a book that you've been sitting on, consider contacting us to put it all together!

As 2025 comes around, we're hoping to rejuvenate our online workshop series with more knowledge-sharing, to host more in-person events to create safe trans spaces together, and to double-down on our 'do whatever projects we can muster' ethos. Enjoy the addition of Mx Bandit comics to this publication - I will be avidly working on more comics and sharing them on Patreon as they are made! I hope that you will join us in whatever way you can, and that you sleep with the perfect temperature of pillow each and every night.

Love & solidarity,
Dorian Rose xo

Index

Comics

Mx Bandit	1
Lucas Califano	3

Art

Leonardo Rizzi	6
Darynkover	7
Ants and Teeth	9
Lee Oakley	10
Dean Williams	12

Poetry

METAMORPHOSIS	15
JEALOUSY IS UGLY / TRANS IS BEAUTIFUL	17
Gender Affirmation	19
Skin and Cotton	20
Shopping List	21
Clapham Stabbing	22
Ode to the fictional trans woman inbound	24
	25
gender free	26
The eventual execution of her (ftm coming out)	28
Cleaning tables	29
Deadname	30
Keep it Moving.	31
Incipience	32
Cosa scorre nelle mie vene?	33
What runs through my veins?	34
The boy I always was	36

Short Stories & Monologues

2023.07.07 [transcribed by archivbot3.0 on 2105.11.01]	37
The Stare of a Silent Star	44
A Town Called Murmuration	54
Braided	58
A satire on pregnancy	62
Butch-to-Butch	65

Essays & Articles

Trans Lives in Early Film	68
TERFism, Transphobia and the 2024 Paris Olympics	73
Film Review: Trailblazers (2024, Sobia Bushra)	79
Film Review: Orlando, My Political Biography (2023, Paul B. Preciado)	82

Call for Submissions — 90

About Transmuted — 91

Crossword — 93

MX BANDIT'S GUIDE TO SELF
(AKA MISCHIEF)
by Dorian Rose
@GENEREFUCCERE
1
WEAR YOUR BATTLE ARMOUR BEFORE LEAVING THE HOUSE.
2
POW
XXzXy
CRACK
BEAT UP YOUR LOCAL NEMESIS + STEAL THEIR LUNCH MONEY!
PUT ONE FOOT IN FRONT OF THE OTHER. FOLLOW THEIR COSMIC WILL.
3
GOVERNMENT
DOLE MUNNY
MR BANDIT, U HAV Ø MUNNY THIS MONTH BC WE H8 RACCOONS!!!
4
CRACKLE
GOVERNMEN
TOSS
NEVER LET CAPITALISM TELL U WHAT YOU'RE WORTH..!
+ DON'T LET BAD TIMES MAKE YOU...
FOOD BANK
5
CAN I GET IT FOR YOU ?
HNNG
LOSE FAITH IN THE GOOD.

CARE
DO THE LITTLE THINGS THAT MAKE YOU HAPPY,
KSSSH
graffito stuff
WOW
NO MATTER HOW FRIVOLOUS THEY MIGHT SEEM.
6
JOIN THE WORKFORCE
NO
FROM EACH ACCORDING TO THEIR ABILITY...
TO EACH ACCORDING TO THEIR NEED.
7
LEARN FROM THE WISDOM OF THE BANDITS OF OLD...
ARR MATEY!
AYE.
AYE.
AYE!
HELL YEAH!
ENGAGE IN COMMUNITY WHEN YOU CAN + HELP EACH OTHER MOVE FORWARD.
HAVE YOU GOT THE KILLER BEES?
THEY ARE READY AND WAITING, BANDIT.
SHOULDN'T WE GET SOME CROCODILES TOO?
ALL THOSE IN FAVOUR OF CROCODILES SAY AYE.
NOO!
RUN! THEY HAVE BEES!
SIC 'EM, COMRADES!
CRUNCH
AND MOST IMPORTANTLY, NEVER PUSH YOUR LIMITS!

Comics by Lucas Califano
@genitaliapanic (insta)

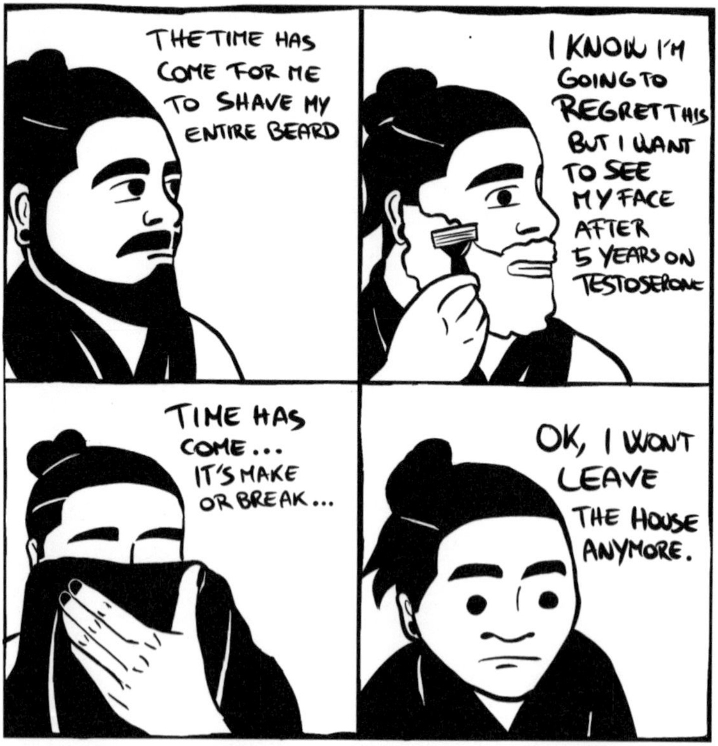

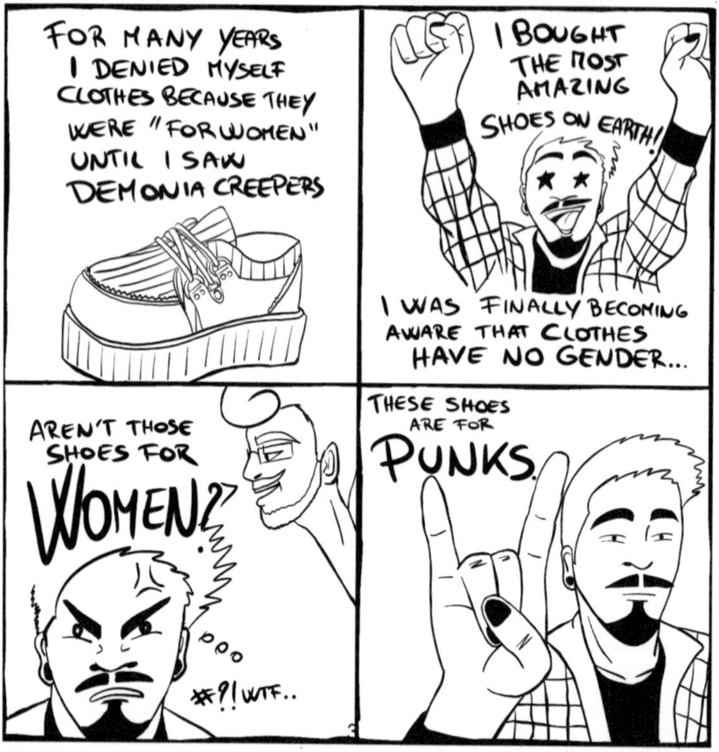

WHY DO WE HAVE TO FIT INTO SOCIAL STANDARDS DECIDED BY OTHER PEOPLE?	IT SEEMS LIKE THEY WANT US TO DO A CLONE WARS REMAKE
HETEROSEXUAL CISGENDER NEUROTYPICAL WHITE ABLED SKINNY PRETTY WEALTHY BINARY	HOW BORING!

Comics by Lucas Califano @genitaliapanic (insta)

NEURODIVERGENT FOLK'S SOCIAL BATTERY CAN GO FROM THIS **90%** TO THIS **1%** SO QUICKLY THAT IT'S HARD TO SEE IT COMING...

ON THE OTHER SIDE, NECESSARY CHARGING TIME IS MUCH SLOWER

IN ORDER TO REDUCE ALL THE ACCUMULATED OVERLOAD

SOCIALIZATION
TOO MANY NOISES
TOO MANY EMOTIONS
BUSY SCHEDULE
TOO MANY STIMULI
OVERTHINKING
STIMMING ABSENCE
EXCESSIVE LIGHTING
MASKING

GENITALIA PANIC

Comics by Lucas Califano
@genitaliapanic (insta)

Lucas Califano aka Genitalia Panic is a Queer Graphic Artist based in Italy. [...] In April 2023 he published his first comic collection in Italy "Fumetti Liberi dal male" [...] On April 2024 Lucas started to translate in English his comics on tapas creating the web series "Free from evil comics" hoping to reach queer, neurodivergent and allies folks around the world. You can also see Lucas' comics on Webtoon (see *Webtoons*, Free From Evil Comics).

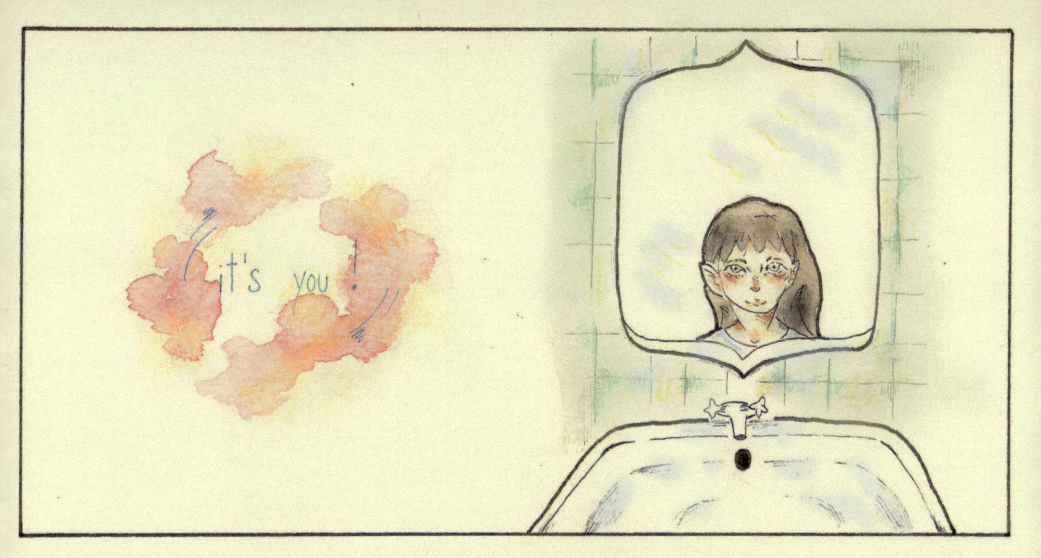

by Leonardo Rizzi / @il_collettivo_(insta)

Love me with all your queerness.

by Darynkover
@darynkover_ (insta)

by Darynkover
@darynkover_ (insta)

by Ants and Teeth
@antsandteeth (insta)

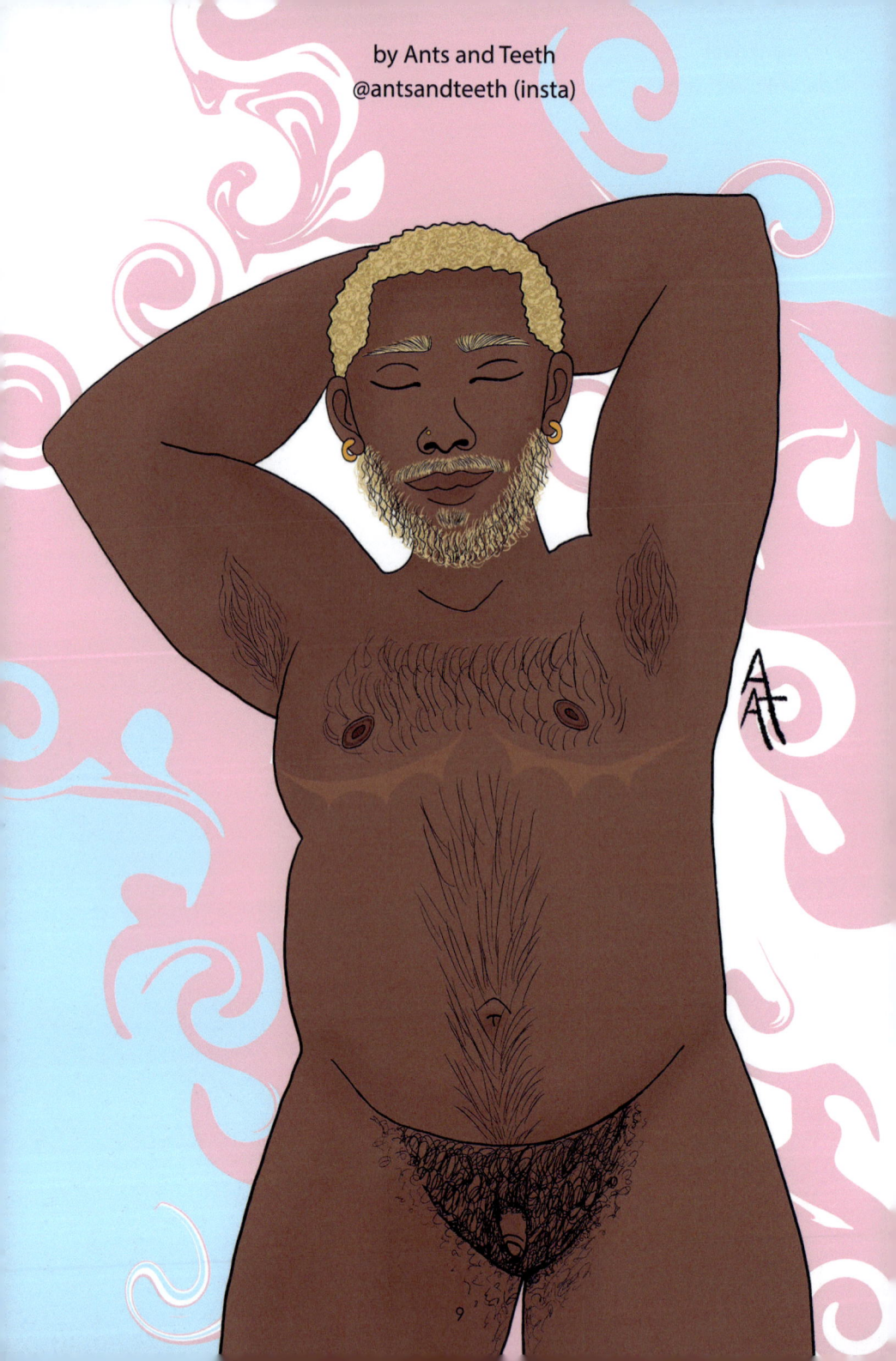

Lee Oakley

"This is heavy and I heard you had space" (2024)

This is heavy and I heard you had space
@oakleeart (insta)

This is heavy and I heard you had space
@oakleeart (insta)

Dean Williams
@kinkleeds (insta)

Dean Williams
@kinkleeds (insta)

Page 6 - Leonardi Rizzi

"I've been thinking a lot about my child self. What would they say about me now? Would they like how we turned out? I wish I could somehow talk to them, but in a way, they are me and I am them. So maybe, just maybe, they're happy as well even if our life isn't perfect."

Page 7 & 8 - Darynkover

"Love me: this piece portrays the love and queer joy I feel from being in a relationship with my partner who's also trans. We don't look like this at all from the outside but our insides are. I hope all trans folks who see this might reflect on their love with their cherished ones and celebrate it. Creature: This is me as a monster. My scars, all of them making me myself . Long hair and a weird smirk. Strange posture and body. The eyes of the ones who dared look at me now sewed on my skin always with me. This is me, as my rage."

Page 9 - Ants and Teeth

"*Trans Joy* is a digital painting of a naked trans man feeling euphoria within his own body. The background is a representation of the happy swirly feelings of gender euphoria."

Page 10 & 11 - Lee Oakley

"Oakley's work *This is heavy and I heard you had space* (2024) explores how the public gaze and societal scrutiny can force the queer community, those with disabilities, and women into a forced performativity. Through their installation, Oakley's sentient work performs the oppression it is grounded by, confronting the viewer with a role-reversal."

Page 12 & 13 - Dean Williams

"The queer scene doesnt have many dedicated safe spaces for NSFW pictures without the expectation for more (think man with a camera stereotype). [...] I want to help cultivate an environment where we don't need to fit into the mould. Credit to @maxiejane and Kongo."

an extract from the zine
METAMORPHOSIS
---

by T Southwell
@t.so_thwell (insta)

Content Note: discussion of sadness & pain (gestures towards unaliving)

It's hard to wake up. I say affirmations but they feel like lies.
It pains me to be dishonest.
It's hard to carry on living when there's no end in sight.
They say it's about the journey not the destination but what if both hurt?
What do you offer?
What do I offer?
What do I
I have nothing for the world and it has nothing for me I should cut
my losses but I have a gambling streak hope must still reside
somewhere within me but I don't know where.
I worry what would happen if I did.

I can only seem to write at the worst times, the times when
everything hurts and the tears well and the walls are closing in
and there is nothing stopping me but I still can't breathe
and I dream of not feeling.

Was my sadness manufactured or was I born with it?
Why must I resign myself to living?

Save me from myself
Save me from this pain
Save me from this world
Save me from my thoughts
Save me from what I want

Leviticus 5.3

sleep with dogs and rise with fleas

The self is impermanent. This person is already dead.
I once existed. Will you remember me?

I wrote a eulogy for myself.
If I've not sinned why am I punished?

Use me
Use me
Use me
Use me
Give me value
I just want to be something

Words are never enough my blood must be spilled
and my bones powdered.
You must eat my flesh.
Only then shall you know my pain.

TAKE THIS ALL OF YOU, AND EAT OF IT,
FOR THIS IS MY BODY,
WHICH WILL BE GIVEN UP FOR YOU

thoughts scrambled
destructive interference
where is my land of milk and honey?

False prophets. My misery was not foretold.

Do not conflate my suffering with progress. There is no virtue.

JEALOUSY IS UGLY / TRANS IS BEAUTIFUL

by Lyd Arlo
@lydarlo (insta)

ONE DAY I WILL FEEL LOOSE FABRIC TO MY CHEST...

I stare into your soul as if it were my own,
Just to calm myself down,
Because I see so much of myself in you,
Or maybe it's the other way around.

But just sometimes...
Your joy reminds me of my pain,
And I look inside myself
Because I know you're not to blame.

I cannot say I am proud of where my mind goes,
But my body grows tired of hiding its shape behind clothes,
One day I will feel loose fabric to my chest,
on that day I will allow myself to forget

All the times I cried over your image,
Longed for it to be mine,
I will realise you as part of my lineage,
It just might take some time.
I know there is a word for this,
but when I call it jealous, I am ashamed.
Envy sends me into crisis,
But what you have- I need the same.

I am so proud of you,
So happy for you,
So unbelievably in awe of your resilience,
But I want that too,
I need that too,
And your experience, holds so much significance.

I stare into your soul as if it were my own,
Just to calm myself down,
Because I see so much of myself in you,
Or maybe it's the other way around.

Gender Affirmation

by Devin Kane
@devinkane.art (insta)

Skin and Cotton

By Devin Kane / @devinkane.art (insta)

A curtain of fabric over skin and fat.
Subtle imitation of what you wish were fact.
Taped into place, space for material sway,
Still tight enough to keep at bay,
Inconsolable feelings of discontent.
They call it incongruence, your body's proprioceptive lament.
Comforted by soft touch of cotton,
Are these pieces of you, you long to be forgotten.

How can you forget?
How can you make *them* forget?

If they promise to forget, are you willing to have the pieces revealed?
Curtain of cotton, fabric from fat, back it is peeled.
Sing your lament to a stranger,
Sing louder than the accusations of predatory danger,
With the words that these do not belong to you.
Hope and pray that they deem your declaration true,
That they confirm your sanity, mental clarity.
In lieu of making you public example of unholy depravity.

So now what?
Is this all there is to do?

Conceal your complexities when you ask them kindly,
To trade, for their silence, your money.
Fork it out, tough it out,
Even if you do, they'll still tell you to get out,
Demand that, for their tolerance, you remain grateful,
Warn you that there's still plenty more ways to make you vulnerable.
You, the forever forgotten, last to be prioritised.
When do we help the demonised?

Shopping List

Axel / @axelh1991 (insta)

Content Note: mild gore

Grapefruit x2

Sugar

Needle and thread

Monster energy (?)

It is summer now. I can feel the sun beating down on my clothed back. Freckles materialise across my forehead—a cluster of stars hidden by the fringe I cut myself last week at 4:30 am, with only the sunrise as my witness. My binder sticks to my chest like honey to my fingertips after breakfast. My ribs ache. I press my fingers between them. Wonder if this is what St Sebastian felt like, arching from his crimson blanket whilst the Holy Irene pulled arrows from his body.

I wonder what Irene thought when she saw him tied to that tree by his wrists, razor wire cutting into his skin. When she saw his face: pain mixed with glorious ecstasy.

When she pulled the arrows from his chest he moaned, no longer burdened by their weight. Did she still think him desirable? Holy? A martyr? After everything?

I'd read you this poem, St Sebastian, but it wouldn't be in my voice. Not yet. Not now. You were a martyr for religion. I am a martyr for myself.

Clapham Stabbing

Two Men Injured in Homophobic Attack

Hamish Bell

Content Note: discussion of grief, homophobia, transphobia, violence, and unaliving.

In the church, at your funeral
Your brother spoke about how he would
Follow you to the bathroom, at pubs
And clubs and bars,
Just to make sure that you made it back alive.
I'd thought, then, bitter, that bathrooms
Weren't the issue –
Your bedroom was what we
Should have been looking out for
But two months later,
Two gay men are stabbed
On your high street. Just
For being gay,
And for standing
On the high street.

Just for standing
In a gay club,
Near the gay bathrooms,
Being gay,
On the high street
Near the church, where your brother
Spoke
At your funeral.
There are no words to make this pretty.
But you were –
Under the lights at the music bar next door –
Bull-headed, walking me home
Past midnight in skirts and a corset,
Insisting that you would be fine.
You were not fine. It was, in fact,
Your bedroom
Not the bathrooms,
In the end.
But it kills me to know
Your brother could have told that story
At your funeral –
Near the high street
And the gay club –
All the same.

Ode to the fictional trans woman

By Anemone

O, Poison,

Whose identity was born out of hatred and ignored for decades

Lend me your strength and your neon pink hair.

O, Ticker, whose transness was made into trivia, in a dusty old wiki

Lend me your love and your words that melt hearts.

O, Bridget, who was robbed of self affirmation, from the moment she found herself

Lend me your style and your sick trickz.

Most of all, lend me your patience

So that I may live another day without being jailed

For doing bad things to a cis writer.

inbound

By M Devenny / @megandevenny (insta)

There's these balloons on my chest

And a feral patch

Dark hair coarses

But there's these lumps of flesh

I am so close, cultivated

But girl hood clings

Painted nails, hair and jewellery

Won't simply cut it

It won't hide the mess

Your back aches,

so your clothes can't cling

There's these balloons on my chest

gender free

By Cyril W Chen / @cyberspacevoid (insta)

I wish I was free
from the roots
—which tether
—--- and ground me ….for…
Maybe I wasn't meant for the Sky
but just the Earth instead

Because I will always be associated with how I look
For better or worse
If only I can be unperceivable
But to live is to be seen

We take these physical bodies
and we do what we can with them
they are our blessing and curse
But more importantly
our shared responsibilities

To the extent where my body is mine
and yours is yours
please never tell me what you
think I should be
Our trans bodies are sacred

By Aspen Greenwood / @ aspen_thetree_greenwood (insta)

In a realm where ideas of perfection reign supreme,
We bear the burden of flaws unseen.
Within, battles rage, silent and willing,
Trapped in cycles of society's billing.

A tax upon our minds, taking up space that is ours.
Instead of the beauty of our mind having the room for flowers -
Whispers of norms echo in our minds,
Making mould like shadows unkind.

But listen, dear heart, to this refrain,
Your value transcends society's domain.
Embrace your truth, with flaws in tow,
For they're the seeds from which courage grows.

Shatter the chains of doubt's cruel prism,
Let your spirit soar with inner truths and wisdom.
Let the garden of the mind flourish -
And those who are doubtful of this may perish.

Life isn't what it was and is what it is,
For that is the cycle of analysis,
Becoming, changing and becoming again.
This process stops only at the end.

The eventual execution of her (ftm coming out)

By Jay Alexander / @jay_2263 (insta)

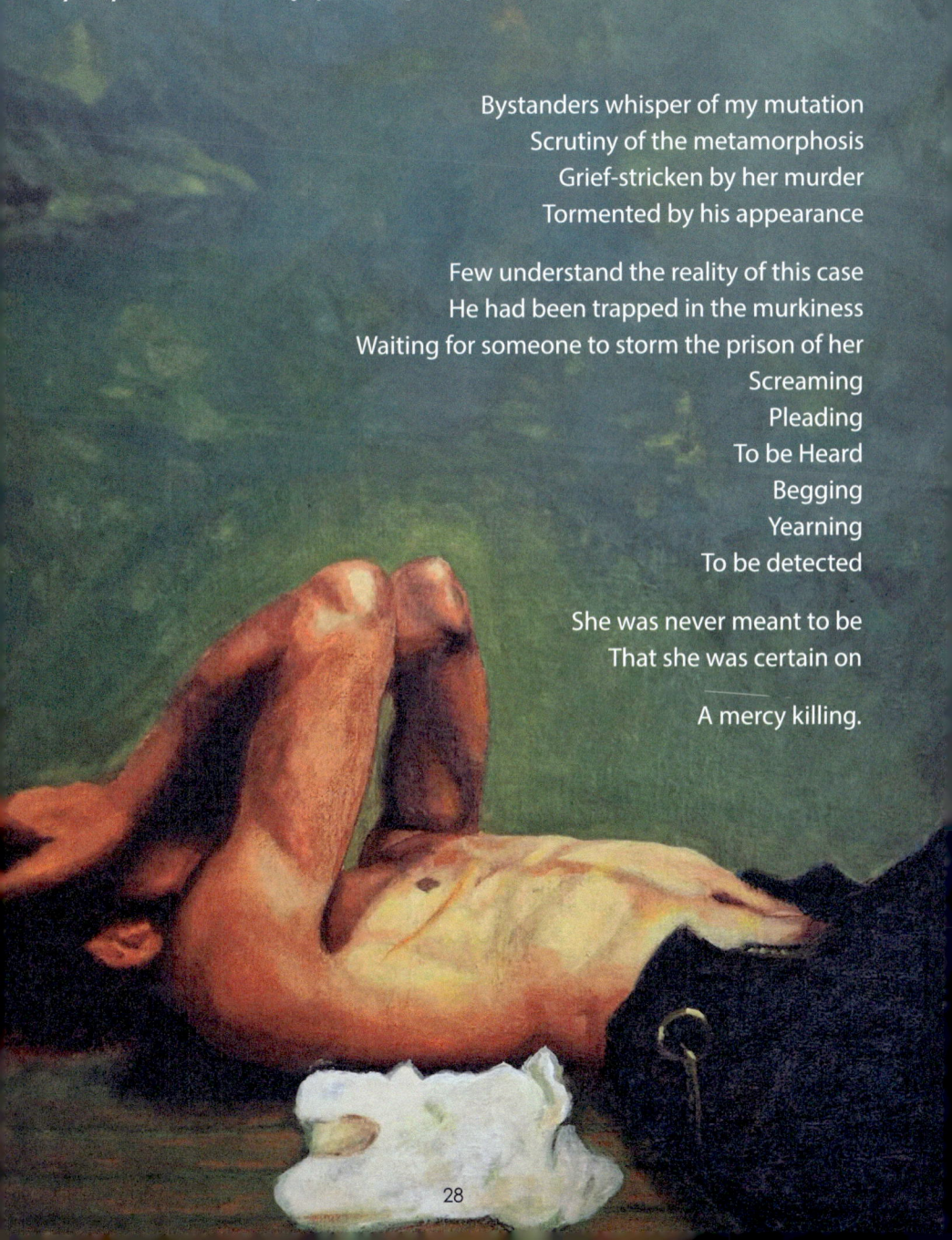

Bystanders whisper of my mutation
Scrutiny of the metamorphosis
Grief-stricken by her murder
Tormented by his appearance

Few understand the reality of this case
He had been trapped in the murkiness
Waiting for someone to storm the prison of her
Screaming
Pleading
To be Heard
Begging
Yearning
To be detected

She was never meant to be
That she was certain on

A mercy killing.

Cleaning tables

By Nancy Boy / @nancyboy.poetry (insta)

Content Note: includes reference to sex & periods.

All night I lick your upper lip from the inside
The thickness: a petal, the peel of a ripe apricot, a beetle vibrating before taking flight
Busy doing something I'm not doing I work
With my hands touching something else
Your chest wounded, scratched, bound
The secret places where skin becomes soft therefore holy
Your skin
Allergic to anything, sight and touch, not glass but crystal
You want my hands cold
How tough
For you to battle a body that bleeds, that opens, that makes you do something you don't like
For me to hold down your wrists, stop
I caress the table (christ), I caress the forks (christ of the scars), I caress you (christ of the scars, protect us)
Too near too beautiful you fall from my eyes, eluding me, crushing me
Love is tough
You and I love with closed fists without having hands

Deadname

By Ari / @arislittleartspace (insta)

Today, I am deadname.

At re-introduction, deadname is the sound of clashing cutlery,
The assault of knives and forks hitting the kitchen drawer,
That pause you take to cringe as you wait for it to finish.

For a while now, deadname has been gravel against flesh after fall,
The peeling of skin from the knee as blood begins to pool,
The automatic smile "It's okay. I know. You'll get it wrong sometimes".

At work, deadname is someone else entirely,
A multicoloured tower built from mismatched Lego bricks,
The necessary clicks to ensure this creation doesn't crash to the ground.

But today, today deadname is a breath of relief,
The sea air of my childhood filling up my lungs,
The salt in my hair from the piers you once took me to.

Today, deadname is the only recording I have of your voice,
One of those daffodils you watered with ocean air and rosewater,
Grown in the garden you fertilised with your body.

So today, I am deadname.
Today, I am grown and I am proudly yours.
But tomorrow, I am who knows, who cares.
Tomorrow, I am growing and I am proudly mine…

Keep it Moving.

By Bea Woods / @way_to_bea_me (insta)

Anxiety dissolved in a dizzying sense of clarity.

The precarious state of livelihood feels like fairytale told to twins.

Coming to as a consciousness in your mid twenties has a habit of shining a light on your shadow. Neurological finesse comes in routine, pills and patches.

Two months to catch yourself in a fall.

Three months to find focus in old, now unfamiliar comforts.

Security and reliability has never felt so wrong.

Two lives lived.

It fades.

Unrecognizable. Polished.

New fuel, still the same fallible machine.

Incipience

By Oli

Content Note: smoking, mention of its harm.

I take comfort in a cigarette, its thin, amorphous vapour pooling around my nostrils. Watchful eyes in raised brows and whispers so crushing I turn and face the wall. A hitch in my ribs startles a cough, eyes burning wide like sight into the sun. One hand pressing against my diaphragm, the other nursing whatever's left.

When the ash flickers, curling and dropping, the smoke, circular, traces the outline of the cig before turning upwards into a veil of grey. Never shaped, or named, or declared as a thing, any thing. Taken by a slight breeze that smells of salt.

I take comfort in knowing things do not wish to be any thing. In the shapelessness of the brewing smoke I kill myself with, or the smoke from a chimney, or a mist drawn from a cold mouth, or the exhaust that sits on the tarmac, stifled. Each colourless shade meeting a cloud and sinking into their nothing nature.

In turn, I am formed of vapour, a nothingness carrying everythingness. I billow, and peel a hangnail from my finger. My eyes on my hands, feeling eyes on my neck, waist, chest, hair, like I was a smog risen from some factory. Some lean forward, unashamed in their glances, peer at me through the looking glass. I catch steel glances, pocket them, I know they have made their opinion.

Cosa scorre nelle mie vene?

By Eglantine Vltava / @eglantine.vltava (insta)

Due litri di acqua, sette grammi di sodio, un po' di zucchero
E anche… tutto quello che ho mangiato, tutto che ho bevuto.

Ho mangiato le verdure vicino le raffinerie
Cadmiò, piombo, vanadio
Ho bevuto il latte sotto l'inceneritore di Acerra
Mercurio, diossine, furani
Ho respirato l'aria dei vicoli
Zinco, cromo, bisfenolo
Ho fatto il bagno nel golfo
Uranio, PFAS, PCB

E adesso, cosa scorre nelle mie vene?
Nel mio sangue scorre la terra contaminata
Nel mio sangue scorre il mare avvelenato
Nel mio sangue sedimentano i fanghi di Bagnoli
Nel mio sangue sbocca la foce del Sarno
Nel mio sangue brucia la Terra dei fuochi

Nel mio sangue scorrono anche due cento picogrammi di estradiolo per millilitro
Nel mio sangue, non scorre più il testosterone

L'estradiolo, me lo sono iniettato io
Me lo sono iniettato nei bassi, in vicoli bui, sotto i sorrisi complici delle puttane e sotto le immagini della Vergine

Il mio seno è cresciuto
La radioattività si è accumulata nei miei capelli
I miei testicoli si sono atrofizzati
Gli idrocarburi contaminano i miei grassi
Il mio viso si è arrotondato, le mie cosce allargate

I metalli si sono fissati nelle mie ossa
Trecce d'argento si sono formate nei miei capelli

Sulla mia schiena, sono cresciute le ali

Mi chiamate mostro, mi dite intossicata
Mi chiamate prodotto di laboratorio, mi dite malata
Ma cosa ha avvelenato il mio sangue,
Quello che ci inietto io
O gli scarti del vostro secolo?

What runs through my veins?

By Eglantine Vltava / @eglantine.vltava (insta)

Two liters of water, seven grams of sodium, a little sugar
And everything else. Everything I ate, everything I drank.

I ate the vegetables near the refineries
Cadmium lead vanadium
I drank the milk near the Acerra incinerator
Mercury dioxins furans
I breathed the air in the alleys
Zinc chromium bisphenol
I swam in the Gulf
Uranium PFAS PCB

34

And now what is running through my veins?
In my blood flows the contaminated earth
In my blood flows the contaminated sea
In my blood sediment the sludge from the Bagnoli steelworks
In my blood flows the Sarno river
In my blood burn the landfills of the Land of Fire

In my blood flow 200 picograms of estradiol per milliliter
In my blood, testosterone no longer flows

I injected myself with estradiol
I injected it in windowless rooms, in dark alleys, under the complicit smiles
of whores and under the images of the Virgin Mary.

My breasts have grown
Radioactivity accumulates in my hair
My testicles have atrophied
Hydrocarbons have contaminated my fat
My face has rounded, my thighs have widened
Metals have set on my bones
Silver braids formed in my hair
Wings sprouted from my back

You call me a monster, you call me intoxicated
You call me lab product, you call me sick
But what has poisoned my blood,
The hormones I inject in it
Or the waste of your century?

The boy I always was

By Karsten / @dragepust (insta)

The boy I always was
Didn't get to play
He got stuck behind a tree
Couldn't talk
Couldn't be

The boy I always was
Didn't have a name
Hadn't ever been
Never heard
Never seen

The boy I always was
Didn't get to be
Those toys are for girls
They said to me
The body's a girl's
I had to be a girl
In everybody's eyes
It was all I ever heard
Naturally I deduce
As a girl I am of use

How could I ever know
That the boy I always was
Was forced to hide away
In a too tight dress
And a skin that didn't fit
No choice
No voice

The boy I always was
Hid behind his walls
Of flowers and glitter

And dresses and silk
And everybody said
He's got to be a girl
His temperament his wishes
His ways and his face
Are those of a girl
All we see is a girl
So no one ever asked
What he thought of himself

But the boy I always was
Wasn't defined by his ways
Or his wishes or traits
He just was
Because he is
And he kept himself lost
And thoroughly hidden
To ease
To please

The boy I always was
Is going to be
Because now I know
That only I am me
I do have a voice
And with that a choice
To be what I am
And not some Madam
I have found myself out
No traces of doubt
Too long I ran

Now I'm a man

2023.07.07 [transcribed by archivbot3.0 on 2105.11.01]

By Brooks K Eisenbise/ @eyesnbyes (insta)

This (assumed) letter was discovered by University of Michigan PhD Candidate in Environmental Tragedy Erid Angret during zer study of Westnedge Hill (Kalamazoo, MI's last remaining intact land mass). According to Angret, it was "among a collection of waterlogged items inside a wooden box. This box was found in the partially flooded basement of an abandoned Arts and Crafts-style home on the west side of Westnedge Avenue. While not relevant to my work studying the Second Lake Michigan Meteotsunami of 2073, this letter may be of interest to those studying the history and lives of Michiganders in the early twenty-first century." Angret also noted that this was the only piece of ephemera within said collection in this handwriting.

Archivist's note: Words and phrases originally underlined for emphasis have been italicized for clarity. There were a lot of underlines.

Hi. It's been a while.

I should thank you for your message, and apologize for waiting so long to write you back. I should, and I would if I were still the person you remember from five summers (or ten years) ago. But I'm not grateful, and I'm not sorry — when I said I couldn't stand your cold and unpredictable gusts of conversation any longer, I meant it. My heart is a slow cooker whose contents oxidize and rot from your lid-lifting. I ask that after you receive this letter, you leave me to stew.

(I'm glad that I no longer have to pretend that my bitterness, self-flagellation, retrophilia, and headache-inducing verbosity make me any worse than human; and that I no longer have to pretend that one 2am text message from you can even begin to bridge the gap between your reality and mine.)

Let me start by sharing some things I *am* sorry for. I'm sorry for curdling your feelings about the dumb little hill we grew up on, the soft wooded place overlooking our town. I'm sorry for showing up as a specter on that hill, strolling in the shadows of the alley by your parents' garage or eating shit on roller skates in front of their house. You deserve peace as much as this ghost does, and I'm glad someone performed the séance that spirited me across Lake Michigan to somewhere new.

I'm sorry for seeing your childhood home as more than a house, and seeing you as more than a person. I'm sorry for tangling you up in the mundane symbology that once kept me alive, the saudade I now only indulge in as a pastime. (I'm doing so now; I hope you'll forgive me.) I was wrong to turn my summer with you into a soliloquy, a narrative I wrote by candlelight without your editorial input; and I was wrong to let it break my heart like a good story always does.

•••

This isn't to imply that I set out to write us into a fairytale romance. I knew from the beginning that you didn't love me the way I'd seen in the movies. (Nor I you, although I tried my damndest.) That whole summer, I was waiting for you to tell me so, to get down on one knee and propose that we find new people to hold. You never did; you kept pulling at my strings until I had wholly unraveled, a once-warm sweater now sitting in a spindly heap around your feet. I made a meal of your hollow romantic notions; I put them into jars and pickled them until they got too sour to stand. It seems you regret it now — how you wrapped your apathy in crepe-thin promises — but I'm left with these shelves of your rotting words.

And I knew about her; of course I did. I knew the way one knows without knowing, the way I saw my father pull up to the house, his 2012 Toyota Corolla filled to the ceiling with blankets and bankers boxes, and knew that my life had been changed. The headlights of your love for her flashed into my eyes the day you came home from that mid-month road trip and didn't look at me, just sliced the thick air with your switchblade as you told your parents that San Francisco missed them. They blinded me when I repeated her name three times like Betelgeuse and you turned ghostly white, guilt-colored. They cut through me the night I reached up to touch you and you slapped my hand away, spreading my thighs and working within me like a third-shift mechanic. She glowed in you — your body an empty church, your eyes south-facing cathedral window images of the Virgin Mother — and I knew, and it filled my throat with bile and my mind with pictures of heart-shaped sunglasses, and I pretended I did not know.

Ours was a summer of heavy silences. You knew that there were secret things I stored in my chest, in my solar plexus, in place of a womb. (You called me the Human Pregnant Pause and your words struck me like a fist.) There, they bloomed and fermented and festered. They flowed through my hands and became sentences in shaky handwriting and pencil marks on craft store paper. You said you wanted to know, but what scraps you saw scared you.

Let me scare you a little more. For old time's sake.

You know about the portrait I drew of you from that move-in day photograph: deep black tracing your aquiline nose on cardboard-colored paper, your curls contoured by a bright green halo; your favorite color creating the shape of you. (Did you keep it? If I dug through your parents' garbage bins — always the archeologist — would I find it there?)

But you don't know that I also sketched you while you slept. Just the one time, with a care and reverence I would have called tender and you would likely call obsessive. I cursed my mechanical pencil for squeaking as I crosshatched your still, sunblushed [sic] face, your matted chestnut curls cherub-like in the early May sun. I marveled at your shoulders, lean and pancaked into the pillow but still rounded and gleaming like armor. You were peaceful and smooth like stone, your body softened edges around something strong. My own body, my personhood too, was like sand, appearing solid but ready to crumble at your touch, disappear through your fingers; there was no core to me. I longed to borrow a piece of yours, if you'd let me.

...

You also don't know how much time I spent lying on the Crane Park tennis courts, feeling the forest-colored sun-warmed cement cook my back and imagining being buried there under cool moist soil. The landscape was changing that summer: mounds of sand taller than two of me punctuated the horizon, and construction barrels rose from the upturned ground like oblong pumpkins ready for Halloween harvest. I floated among the dusty green, unmoored and waiting for my childhood backdrop to become unrecognizable.

By Brooks K Eisenbise

I was half-convinced that before the summer was through, the tennis courts — that rendezvous spot we claimed before we knew Lorde had sung about it, that box whose chain-linked walls your sister and I scaled blind drunk on five-dollar-vodka screwdrivers — would be buried under soft loam the way my lanky boybody [sic] had begun to bury itself under layers of progesteronated [sic] womanfat [sic], leaving a grassy knoll in its place, a grave without a headstone.

You can't have known that for me, being smothered by my own curves by an unconcealable femininity I suddenly despised was a fate worse than blanket-close earth-wet death; that I would grab at my hips and stomach and thighs in the shower until the flesh I didn't want was encircled by the blood-flushed crescent moons of my nail indentations, a skin-suspended ecliptic. I never told you about the night I spent on the bathroom floor of my student apartment in Copenhagen with a Sharpie and a throat full of curses, writing messages to you on the parchment of my body. *RUN FROM ME, SAVE YOURSELF, NOT ONE STEP CLOSER*, begged the black letters I wrote on the places my clothes would cover, as if you weren't already four thousand one hundred and sixty one miles away; as if you hadn't already been saved by someone new.

Bury me with the tennis courts, make me structurally sound, of invisible use, I prayed. You don't know how much I prayed that summer.

...

I could fill a book with things you do not know, and I did for a while. I kept a journal of the feelings that boiled and bubbled out of me, scalding hot and too alive to house in the hollows of my body. I promised myself that I would not show you this book unless I had won you fully and forever. (What were we to each other but prizes, objects? What was a relationship but a trophy given to the desirable, the normal, the blessed?)

I charted our saga like a fangirl's viral Tumblr post, romanticizing five years of panic attacks and closed-mouth kisses and bone-shaking horniness that defied fidelity and curfew. I molded my pain into poems, hoping that in their lyricism you would forgive me for being hurt by your broken promises, your date-night delinquency, your many-edged words that cut me like paper, quick and bloodless and stinging. I wrote you letters I never sent, nauseating myself with the sentimentality of the act, communicating with some future version of you who could see my correspondence as more than naïve and terrifying devotion.

Those letters, that notebook, the ticket stubs from movies we watched stiffly without touching hands, live in a box under my bed. Sometimes I wonder where they would be now if I had given them to you. Would they be in your own hidden box, the one where you keep offerings from your exes? Has your girlfriend rifled through that box's contents, just like I did when I found it all those years ago, attempting to create a narrative from Sour Patch Kids wrappers and corner store receipts and Skype messages transcribed in glitter gel pen? Is she feeling that blade between her ribs, just like I did?

I hope not. I hope that, in her world, things are just things.

•••

During, and for some time after, I wondered what I was to you. Was I an old friend? A rebound lover? A ghost haunting your parents' house in panties and your white button-up shirt? You once told me that I looked like an old photograph of someone's grandmother. Is that what I was to you — a captured memory, stiff and static, already fading?

I didn't know it then, but to me, you were the medium through which I could experience boyhood. I studied you like an anthropologist, documenting the curl of your smile, the curve of your nose, the lilt of your laugh. I burned them underneath my eyelids and etched them into brown paper with charcoal pencil. I stood before the picture of you that your father took when you were ten, your angled body and Margaret Keene eyes tinted red in the low light of the late-night living room, and brought it to life in my mind like a zoetrope.

What was he like, this barefoot boy with the woods in his backyard? I sometimes click through your dad's Flickr account searching for the answer, where your baby face frozen in black and white film is shuffled between photos of the man you've become, right eyebrow perpetually cocked like a finger on some sarcastic trigger. How does a boy become a man, and how can I avoid growing up forever, Peter-Pan myself like Mary Martin? These photos provide no answers; they only cut me open the way I expect — right down the middle, flayed.

I wish I saw myself in those photos — in your prepubescent freckles, your piercing green-turned-gray eyes, your sandy hair still pin-straight at the ends. I wish I saw myself in the little boy's shadow you left behind (*Peter Pan* again); instead I jumpscare [sic] myself with an image of my own slim teenage-girl shoulders, my excess hair condensed and discarded behind haphazard victory curls. Your father called that photo *A Walk in the Park*; I wouldn't have, but the art is never permitted to title itself.

"The view from behind her is distinctly American," comments some stranger on the Flicker post that features my façade. Is there something distinctly American about hiding the parts of yourself that you hate; about turning away from the camera, wishing you were born with the face of the photographer's son in place of your own? What's more American than letting womanhood slice the flesh off your bones so that He [sic] has something to consume?

I wonder how I taste. I suppose you know.

...

By the end of it, we were both cowards. You, for failing to tell me that somewhere in the Utah desert, you'd let me go; and me, for failing to share why I couldn't do the same.

I hope you know, that night on the curb in front of my house, spotlit [sic] by the orange glow of a Rose Street lamppost, with the late-August mosquitos biting our ankles raw… I hope you know that your confession, the true answer to the question I posed (*"You've never been sure about me, have you?" "No, I haven't, but I'm sure about somebody else"*), wouldn't have shattered my poor fragile drowning girlheart [sic]. I, too, wanted to be set free. Behind the white Cadillac taking us from our wedding to our honeymoon clattered the tin cans of regret and burden and motherhood and compromise — empty words, his and hers: *I do, I do*. I could hear that car revving its engine in the distance and it filled me with dread.

But this was a game of chicken, and I couldn't give in first. It would unanimously rule my valiant attempt at girl(friend)hood a failure, five years of star-crossed love deemed utter delusion. I couldn't admit to you that I had fashioned my siren song from Lana Del Rey tracks and scraps of your high school girlfriend's enviable femininity, that the girl whose eyes you couldn't meet was nothing more than a character I was tired of playing. You alone had taught me the ways I could matter to a(nother) boy: I was a distraction in a floral print button-up dress, a music taste charity case, a tutee of Bruce Willis' cinematic prowess. I was the silent audience for your restless night guitar riffs.

I couldn't admit that I'd spent five years stuck on you like a shadow and didn't have the strength to slam the bedroom window shut and tear myself away. I guess I needed to hear it from you first: that I wasn't the girl you wanted, a girl ~~worth wanting.~~

•••

If I ended this letter by assuring you that it accuses you of nothing, and that my words are flowing onto the page because they have to, I can't stop them, they're more living than I've ever been, I doubt you'd believe me. Feelings like these look hard as stone, although I know them to be yielding like clay, reshaped by memory and fantasy and years that have doubtless created a chasm between us. Everything seems so much more solid before it's touched.

And if I told you that the bravest thing I've ever done is ask you to stop texting me, to tell you that no, I won't explain to you why your random wyd's tighten the muscles of my neck like a thick leather belt, if I told you that I've never been braver, I bet you wouldn't believe me then, either. Or maybe you would, and you'd pity me — you, who enters the Sprinkle Road on-ramp at one hundred miles per hour for something to do; your Aries-Moon heart will choke your lungs with smoke long before the cigarettes catch up with you.

(Forgive me for waxing poetic at the end here. Yet another thing to apologize for.)

— The Boy You Lost

This transcription and the archival material(s) from which it originated are the sole intellectual property of the University of Michigan Institute of Human-Derived Sensation, Affect, and Self (IHDSAS) Historical Archives. To browse our collection, link your NeuraNode® to our server here.

The Stare of a Silent Star

By Lillian Tomkins / @lilliantomkins (substack)

Content note: gore

I stared silently at the stranger's face. His sharp jawline alit, only apathy in my heart, and his rough stubble scratched at my eyes. His unkempt hair was finally starting to get long, but that mattered little – they would make him cut it soon. His skin was weathered and wrinkled despite his relative youth. His lips were too thin for my taste and his neck strangely too bumpy. Most notably, his stunning blue eyes held no flicker of life. *Why?* I thought, *why does this face make me feel so empty?*

The only detail I felt comfortable being disgusted with was the hairy black tumour growing from beneath his ear. It was normal to hate that – everyone hated their tumours, even if some pretended otherwise. Who could blame anyone for hating a disgusting thing eating away at your life?

I brushed his hair as smooth as I could manage, then slipped away as he pulled on his itchy work overalls. He stood there a while longer, alone to even himself, staring at the mirror. His small, dimly lit room held no furnishings, much like himself, who wore nothing but the plainest threads.

"Adam! Are you done sorting that damn hair out yet?" his father called from downstairs.

…

Adam sat at the ancient hard-wood dining table, his parents at either side of him and the empty seat opposite, staring him down as always. Four plates of boiled meat and potatoes sat at the table. Adam chewed and swallowed his food. It was never enough to satiate his brutish body, even though his father's job earned them more meat than most.

He almost asked, "Mother… could I please have just a little more?"

But he knew how that went. His father would have replied, not moving an inch, "Absolutely not, son. Your little brother gifted us this food – he deserves his share just as much as you."

It was always the same. *Always*. Tears welled in Adam's eyes as he bit at his thin lips. He had not the strength to run through their perfectly-rehearsed argument anymore. Better to just let the show play out in his mind than get trapped on stage yet again…

Adam would cry, "But he *can't eat*. He gets to have never lived while *I* must tend to the seeds he sowed!"

His father would remain impassionate, "Be grateful The Dealer spared you, boy."

His mother would speak not a word from her tumour-ridden mouth, yet would scream with her eyes, 'You were our miracle, why must you make yourself our curse?'

He left to the fields in silence.

…

Adam scratched at his tumour. The pain grounded him. It was all he could really feel. Not the cold mud creeping over his boots, nor his aching muscles, nor the chill mountain breeze. He picked up a potato – a healthy one, finally. It had a smear of blood on it, my blood.

…

As always, I watched Adam spend his lunch alone, at the edge of the village. He could never fit in with the men and the women always treated him like a man.

Their mountaintop plateau sat as a lone island in a sea of clouds. He watched the clouds twist, swirl, undulate and sweep. Within the ceaseless storm shone lights, strange and varied. Solar flares escaped the mist, casting their burning light across the horizon, reaching higher and higher… until the mist swept up to re-capture it. All colours of lightning coiled angrily within and forked at the stars in rage.

The stars above sat still, shining their eternal dusklight – just enough to keep life on the edge of death. A few hundred of them shone brighter than the rest. He hated their judging stares.

"Do you ever wonder what is out there?" I asked, as I often did.

I wish I could stop thinking about it, he thought.

Nothing scared Adam more, yet still he stared out onto the unfathomable.

…

Thirty-nine sleeps later, The Dealer emerged from the mists. I saw them, shambling beneath their cloak of kaleidoscopic blacks, cutting their silhouette from the bone-white mists. My heart skipped and my legs twitched, yet Adam stood still, entranced.

"Ah!" Someone grabbed Adam's arm and pulled. It was John, one of the Elder field workers. He had mud all over him from running across the field. I wondered how many potatoes he had crushed.

"Adam, stop looking at the damn thing! I am not letting another first-born son fuck up our lives again."

Adam followed John back to his home. His mother gave him a long hug – severed short by his father ushering him into his room. His mother only ever hugged him when The Dealer arrived. As always, his father lectured him on the dangers of The Dealer and their mysterious powers. Adam and I just stared at the blood under his nails and speckled on his shoes. It was always there when he rushed from work.

Adam stared into his mirror alone. He did not hear my dramatic complaints – he 'needed' to be numb to survive this. But still he knew what I would say, and so my cries still crept in, *why do you want to meet The Dealer? What do you want to change? What did John mean by 'another' first-born son? I thought I was the only one that The Dealer didn't take…*

He was starting to listen to me.

…

He spent his next lunch staring at the still stars with envy. He could not bear to look at the mists. Against his will, the scripture that had been ingrained in the sediment of his mind flashed to the surface:

'And so The Founder made the First Accord – Every first-born shall be born still, their eye's spark traded for the shine of a star that would feed our crops and light our way.'

He longed to be one of those bright stars, dead and quiet – never cursed with thought. His light could have brought stability, yet his vacant eyes seemed to only cause hurt. His mother had been so happy when The Dealer would not trade for him. She had always wanted a daughter.

One of the stars was his brother, but he knew not which. Not that it mattered, really. *Oh, to die with a purpose and not need to exist…*

…

Adam's father gave him a Lightball as a present, but he didn't really care. They were balls of jelly that absorbed and released starlight. The Dealer traded a Lightball for each joyous memory sacrificed, with its duration relative to the intensity of emotion lost. His father traded recent memories of him being proud of Adam's 'good behaviour'.

The 'gift' just let me see Adam's face in more detail. A repulsive beard had sprouted and began to cover his tumour. He thought that was helping.

…

Three visits from The Dealer and fifty sleeps later, he was back in his room, in the dark. The Lightball had run out. John had dragged him back and Adam's mother was the one to cut their hug short this time. That morning he had argued again.

Adam couldn't look at himself. He had not the strength to squeeze out but a single tear. They built up within him, growing and growing in pressure, weighing his chest and clouding his mind. They boiled within, scarring his insides, numbing his entire being.

And so, he scratched the tumour, spilling my blood upon his body and sheets and floor. I screamed to be free of his nails, but he heard nothing and felt nothing but my pain. He swirled the morning's argument around and around and around in his mind until he collapsed on the floor.

We... Don't know why The Dealer didn't take you.

But there was another first-born son who lived, wasn't there?

Who told you that? They were lying.

John said it when he dragged me back once! I could tell he wasn't lying.

Oh... Do not speak of this.

I deserve to know, father!

You deserve nothing, boy. Your brother died in your place. He deserved a life yet did not get one. You don't know how lucky you are to be alive.

Please please please stop talking about him, this is about me!

Everything is about you, boy, you know not the lengths we go for you.

Tell me then! Tell me why I alone can't be trusted to even look at The Dealer and what happened to the other first-born son. Please.

He... He was the Cursebringer, the Founder's son. His survival of birth turned the village against the Founder. The very man who decreed the First Accord failed to trade his son away! The boy grew up so afraid and isolated from his fellow men, he made a deal for immortality and fled to the mists, never to be seen again. In the coming months, our tumours began to grow. He traded our lives for his. There have been several first-born sons that lived since, but they were all strange and tempted by the mists. They have a habit of asking too many questions. But you are not to tell anyone of this! Only the Elders of fifteen-thousand sleeps are permitted to know this. I only told you to stop you from asking anyone else – to protect you.

…

As Adam dug at dirt, I thought, *there were others – I really am not alone.*

As Adam washed potatoes with muddy hands, my blood still embedded under his nails, I thought, *what really happened to the Founder's son?*

As Adam watched his father go to his job in the hut at the farthest edge of town, I thought, *what does father's job actually involve? What is the blood under his nails?*

How could they possibly make my life worse? Adam thought as he followed after his father.

Only Elders were allowed in the hut, so Adam put his ear to the door crack. He closed his eyes as we listened. There was some sort of distant sawing or cutting…

He opened his eyes and there they were. Black upon black upon white. The Dealer, a few hundred feet away. Nobody else was around.

They saw me.

Adam froze.

The Dealer began to turn away.

"No, wait…" Adam whispered instinctually.

I will WAIT if you ENTER the hut and DO NOT SCRATCH your tumour.

They spoke into our mind and we agreed.

Yes.

The Dealer Bell rang four times, signifying their arrival on the other side of the village. It was tricking them for me. After about fifteen seconds, Adam's father burst out the door, which obscured Adam, to sprint away with desperate speed, leaving the door unlocked.

Adam felt a strange warmth of care from his father as he stared at the Dealer for a few more seconds.

"Adam, go inside!" I shouted at him.

He listened.

It was empty, except for a hatch on the floor that led down into a deep laddered hole. A Lightball illuminated a red chamber deep down. All he could hear was dripping.

Adrenaline carried him down those steps. To truth.

He found an armless man bound in chains to a funnel-shaped floor – everything slick with blood. Slabs of meat hung from hooks while hatchets and saws laid on the table. His arm stumps pumped rivers of blood into a drain beneath him. It felt like my room. The man bore no tumours. He breathed steadily as he slowly looked up to our eyes.

It was like looking into a mirror – we saw ourself in the man's lightless eyes. They reflected a stare of silent stars – the look of death. We saw our own pain. We saw what Adam could become. We saw the man's arms regrow before our eyes, sinew, vein and bone.

The Founder's son had not fled to the mists. He now sat before us, chopped into pieces – into meat. But Adam felt no satisfaction. He felt no anger. He had never felt so numb. He just grabbed a hatchet and drew it to his tumour–

"No!" I screamed at him, "Do *not* give up on me."

The founder's son spoke with monotone distain, "Do it. For your own sake, end your suffering. Get back at *everyone* who made us suffer."

I could do nothing but whisper, "You don't deserve *any* of this. Nobody deserves any of this."

I… Know, he thought, directly acknowledging me for the first time as he dropped the hatchet.

Adam whispered to the dead-eyed man, "You don't deserve any of this... I will get you out–"

"No." He stated in response, "This is what I need. I can't live out there."

"What?" Adam shouted, "You want to stay here, letting them chop you up, letting them *eat* you?"

Adam retched, his numbness shattered by violent convulsions. Speaking his suspicions made them real. Every boring meal of his life had been him. And he only ever wanted more.

"This is my penance and my revenge. I can see in your eyes that you understand."

Adam leant a hand on the bloody table, "But... you can just stop it – you can leave and stop the pain!"

"Then why are you still here?" He asked, wiping wet hair from his eyes with a new hand, "Because you *are* what you know."

It became too much for Adam. His words were going nowhere. They would find him soon.

"Adam... you can't help him here and now. You need to go."

Adam climbed the steps as fast as he could, desperate to escape the grim reflection of his mind, but more so to meet The Dealer. Up and up and– his mother stood at the top of the ladder, her tumorous face twisted in horror. I could not tell if she was expressing empathy or admonishment. Regardless, her tears fell upon his innocence lost.

She helped him out the ladder hole, but wouldn't let go. Adam found himself not caring for her quiet sobbing and futile grasping – she had brought this upon herself, after all. He pushed past her towards The Dealer waiting outside.

WHAT do you DESIRE? Asked The Dealer.

Adam stood silently.

His mother quietly screamed her voice apart as she ran to get others.

"Adam." I said, "You know who you are. You know what I am. I think about it constantly, which means that you do too. It is okay, truly."

His tight muscles relaxed. Everything went quiet.

I am not a firstborn son. I want to be a woman… What will that cost everyone?

It will cost them NOTHING.

What will it cost me?

Your MANHOOD.

So… I lose nothing?

EQUIVALENT EXCHANGE with an individual as all DEALS are.

Everything made sense at once.

The Founder's son… no, the Founder's daughter *didn't sacrifice our lives, she offered you her death in return for life? We are poisoning ourselves with her immortal flesh!*

CORRECT.

"Son, son! Get away from him." Adam's father was screaming. He had been for a while. Everyone was there, the whole village circled around Adam and The Dealer. They were so scared.

Do you ACCEPT the DEAL?

Adam saw his father reach for the hatchet at his back.

"YES!" I cried, immediately falling to the floor in writhing euphoria.

His bones bent, hair melted, skin stretched, clothes ripped and mouth screamed. I tore myself into reality, as raw and bloodied as a newborn. Through my own eyes, I saw each of their contorted faces as they witnessed my most vulnerable of moments. They looked at me as I once looked at my tumour – comfortable in their disgust. I had taken *my* hatchet to *my* body and they were scared.

Tears flowed from my eyes, free and easy, the pressure released. I realised that Adam was never really real, he was a construct, moulded from my soul by the pressure of everyone's eyes. He was dead in all senses of the word – unchanging and cold. And I am life.

"You are all eating a woman. Your society is built on carving her apart." I proclaimed, "Her undying flesh is what kills us, not her deal."

I couldn't help but laugh. It was gone, the apathy in my heart, subsumed by love. My uproarious, defiant laugh rocked the sea of silent stares, whipping waves within society that would never break. In time, their cliffs would crumble. But not yet.

I knew I had done all that I could. They parted as I walked to the edge of the mists – arms wrapped around me from behind, my exit cut short by my mother's embrace.

I savoured the hug, before severing it as I said, "Please remember me as Eve…"

And then I was gone to the mists, certain that others would follow in time.

I am sorry, brother. Your light may no longer reach me, but it burns brighter than ever in my eyes – for now I live for myself.

A Town Called Murmuration

By Rebys J Hynes / @rebysjhynes (insta)

Chlorine Jones (346, all pronouns), adventurer and explorer, passed away peacefully in their sleep last night, surrounded by family and lovers. She was known for her planet-hopping adventures and lavish lifestyle. Xe was born during the Multiverse Wars and went on to fight oppression and tyranny across the seven galaxies. He is perhaps best known for killing the Void King and –

'I was not a 'he' when I killed the Void King! You live all your life being – if I may say so – bloody amazing and then the press don't even have the decency to match the gender to the adventure.'

An hour trek from the raggedy town of Murmuration, on the cowboy planet Clementine, Theta Jones pushed his grampix' hoverchair through the desert. Since the morning broadcasts, Chlorine had done little but complain about the mistakes made by her obituaries.

'You approved them all,' said Theta. 'You said, and I quote, 'I want to see the tear-soaked comments of my adoring public before I pop my clogs!"

'There's a lot of comments but nothing with pizzaz. People are sad, but shouldn't they be devastated? Not a single day of mourning declared on any planet. Can you push a bit harder, son? I want to get there before I die.' Chlorine grumbled. 'They didn't even talk about when I toppled a monarchy and became a queen. Different planets, same day!'

Theta's impulse was to tell his grampix that he had heard all these stories a million times before. Then he remembered that this was the last time he would hear them told like this. From the source.

'It's too hot,' said Theta. 'I haven't seen a single animal since landing on this dustbowl. There's not even a bird in the sky. How do people survive here?'

'I said you'd regret binding for a pilgrimage, but did you listen? Do you know what your problem is, boy? You're too serious. You'll never get a boyfriend if you can't laugh at a shit situation.'

'I already have two boyfriends.'

'Well, you won't get a third!'

They trundled along in silence, until Theta asked. 'Why do you want to become a bird, Grampix?'

'So I can shit wherever I want.'

'Classy.'

'I don't wanna become just *any* bird. I wanna become part of all the birds.'

When his grampix called last week with 'one last request', Theta hadn't expected it to involve travelling across two galaxies to this backwater planet. Chlorine claimed to have finally found it. The Flock. Theta wasn't sure he believed xem. But the cancer covered enough of Grampix's body that Theta couldn't say no to even the wildest of requests. Everyone deserves one last adventure.

'You believe there's a flock of birds flying around the galaxy, pickin' up the souls of the dying and then – what? The souls ascend into birdhood?'

'That's what the legend says.'

'So, the afterlife is being a pigeon?'

'Nothing as mischievous or finite as that. Becoming part of the Flock is not heaven or hell. It's more of a right place, right time sort of situation. If you can track them down, they might consider your application.'

'To become a pigeon?'

'To become a pigeon amongst a flock. Heard there's plenty of legendary trans folk in there. I'll fit right in. My sources say that the Chevalier d'Eon is in there – as a heron! I hope I'm an owl. Would love to turn my head right around."

'And how are you so sure that Clementine is a stop on the Flock's journey?'

'Consider Murmuration.'

'The town? Bit of a dump if you ask me. Looked at us like they'd never seen trans people before. Thought you were wrong to tell me not to bring my stungun.'

'It was named by the birdwatchers who settled here eight-hundred years ago.'

'And?'

Chlorine grinned mischievously. 'C'mon. I can't spell everything out for you when I'm not there.'

'Oh.' The barren sky. 'No birds.'

'Not a single flying animal on this entire planet.'

'Very good.' After a few minutes, Theta asked, 'Why me? You have almost a hundred descendants. You could have called any of them.'

'We stop here!'

Theta let go of the hoverchair.

'I must do the next part alone,' ze declared. 'The Flock do not like the smell of the living.'

'I'm to leave you here to either become a bird or die of heat exhaustion?'

'Off you trot, son.'

Theta sighed. 'I'm going to miss you, Grampix.'

'Bah. You'll see me again.'

'What if you're wrong?'

'What if? Such a lazy question, unless you answer with 'who cares?''

By Rebys J Hynes

'One more story?' asked Theta. 'For old time's sake?'

'Nah. I think I've had enough stories.' His grampix's pronoun badge fluctuated between every option. In the end, Chlorine Jones was going to die as everything they ever were. 'Hey, kidda. Wanna know the truth about all this. Why you? Why I wanna become a bird?'

'Of course.'

'I have lived a long life and I have been so many people. I have lived spectacularly. I have done wonderful things.' He prodded Theta's shoulder playfully. 'But I have yet to fly. I really want to try flying. I reckon, one day, you will too.'

Theta walked back towards the town called Murmuration and, at his Grampix' request, didn't look back. He was close to his ship when suddenly a green crack ruptured through the orange sky, out of which burst more birds than Theta believed the universe could hold. All moving as one. Leading the murmuration, a heron.

The torrent hurled out of town, then thundered back as quickly as it left. Townsfolk flooded the street, crying in awe. Theta couldn't help but join in.

One of the birds shit on his shoulder. He need not look up to know the culprit was an owl.

Braided

By Chandler Carter / @puppetpostin (insta)

Content Note: discussion of religiosity, use of the 'f' word.]

I was 7 years old when I consciously experienced a baptism for the first time. My pastor had a strong hand grasping the shoulder of a teenage boy; another man, whose face I can't quite remember, was accompanying him at the opposite shoulder. The metal tub must have been cold against the boy's knees, his wet basketball shorts clinging to his thighs and the lower half of his t-shirt doing the same to his slightly pudgy midsection. Heads were bowed, occasional "amens" were muttered following particular statements from the pastor, and I was confused but interested nonetheless.

My eldest brother, a neighborhood friend, and myself were gathered around our ancient box TV that sat on the carpeted floor of the back bedroom on a spring afternoon.

"That's fag music!" the boy commented to whatever miscellaneous media was on at the time.

I had heard that word a few times at this point in my life as a barely preteen; my father and his friends had used that word to describe people and things they didn't like. I don't recall what kicked off the conversation after the offhand comment, but I do know it was the first time I had heard of same-sex relationships. It had never occurred to me that that was something that was a possibility; deep down, I know that something clicked for me that day. Both my understanding of what I had internally been experiencing and my immediate fear of the perceived sin ingrained within me.

Judas betrayed Jesus in exchange for 30 pieces of silver. We will never know exactly why he chose to do this, if it was a choice at all. It's easy to blame it on greed and to believe he did it simply in exchange for the money, but maybe it was outside of his own control—an unseen force acting upon Judas to commit the ultimate act of betrayal. During the Last Supper, Jesus hands Judas a piece of bread that he had dipped into a dish, claiming that whoever this piece was handed to would be the apostle to betray him; Jesus knew. It is claimed that Satan entered upon him from the piece of bread. Satan's influence on Judas was mentioned after that point as well, not simply the existence of his mere greed.

Guided back and downwards by strong and holy hands, I watched the boy being submerged in the water of the metal tub. The immersion of the human body along with a spoken prayer is seen as a rebirth or regeneration, the ultimate act of purification. During the time I was witnessing this baptism, I, of course, had no understanding of how such a quick and simple act could be so important and cleansing. I still don't, to be completely honest. All I remember worrying about was if the boy was going to get water up his nose, was he going to be cold for the rest of the church service? Looking back now as an adult who escaped religion, I believe these childish thoughts speak for themselves. Sure, the boy being baptized was a bit older than me, but he was still very much a child. What had any child done that would require such an intense action in the name of purity? If I was impure, it was at the hands of the world around me.

I entered my first relationship with another boy at the age of 13, something that would pave the way for the man I am today. He had dark eyes and dark hair—a consistent type in men for me, apparently—and he smelled like his father's cigarettes. My hands, bitter cold from the rapidly dropping fall temperatures of the evening, gripped his well-worn zip-up jacket and eventually wound wrapped around his thin wrist. I kissed his back—such a small and gentle gesture that I'm not sure he ever even noticed. I spent the following almost three years with him, years I still remember very vividly. The summers were spent on the banks of the little Scioto, bare chests and backs exposed to the sun, and there was no fear of being discovered in such a manner. Winters outside of school were spent in my bed more often than his, with nervous and inexperienced hands roaming tense bodies and mouths sealed tightly in fear of drawing the attention of my parents. He left me in the winter of my sophomore year of high school, hiding his attraction to men from that point forward.

Judas went by himself to the Temple, the priests at the time served as authorities, and Judas agreed to lead them to Jesus in exchange for the seemingly miniscule pieces of silver, something so small in comparison to the life that would be taken. There in the Garden of Gethsemane, Judas kissed Jesus, identifying him to the temple priests. Did Judas regret what he did before he did so? Did he hope that a kiss would permit his forgiveness and show his guilt, his still potentially lingering love for Jesus? Despite his regret, the betrayal was put into motion and could not be taken back after his identification of Christ there in the Garden. Judas attempted to return those 30 pieces of silver, a desperate attempt to reverse his actions, but he was dismissed. Judas left the coins on the floor next to the authorities as they arrested Jesus.

He was brought to the surface mere seconds after being plunged under, but I wonder how long it felt to him. When those arms began to pull him back upwards, the same way they pushed him down, did it feel like a saving grace? Did they feel like the hands of God? Was he clean now? I wonder from time to time if a baptism would have saved me, something my desperate and humiliated brain used to ponder much more often. I struggle with the feelings of being impure, dirty from the hands of multiple lovers over the years, some who were mere strangers; dirty at my own hands as well for changing the body God had supposedly given me. I will never feel the loving hands of the Lord, the strong hands of my pastor against my shoulder, or the submersion of my impure body into icy waters. If I am too sinful for simply being who I am, then I will find love and acceptance in those who don't turn their cheek to my filth.

I am loved unapologetically and without shame now, and I do the same for him. He holds my hand in both public and private, not afraid of what others may think of him and not afraid of who he himself knows he is. This is one of his most admirable traits, and I've been envious of it since I met him. He takes me to family dinners where I am treated as an equal and told to visit again in the future, a promise that I have followed through with. He looks at me as if I'm the most precious thing in his existence, like I'm the center of the universe; he thinks I'm beautiful, and he doesn't have to say it out loud for me to know. I still can't help but look away and wish he'd look anywhere else besides at me, afraid that he'll look a little too long and a little too close and see everything ugly that resides within and upon me. He lets me bury my face into the crook of his neck, my hands slipping beneath his t-shirt, to explore similar imperfections: imperfections that seem so mesmerizing on him but feel so wretched on me. He will continue to look at me with bright eyes and a toothy grin, hands in my hair or against my back, and I will be loved even with my impurities—loved without judgment and without even a second thought.

Judas hung himself from a tree in a Potter's Field after realizing the act of betrayal he had committed, a field that would later be called Hakeldama, or Field of Blood. Judas Iscariot is seen as the ultimate traitor, but we must realize that without the betrayal by Judas, the salvation of humanity at the core of the Christian faith would not have taken place. Judas kicked off this crucial sequence of events: the arrest, the crucifixion, and the subsequent resurrection. Jesus knew what was going to happen, he knew who this act would be done by, and yet he allowed fate to take its course; Yet he loved Judas even with the existence of this preordained knowledge. If we are meant to be completely pure as human beings, then why are we made to commit and carry out such "sinful" acts?

If God is omnipotent and all-knowing, then why was I made to be the way I am? We are given the illusion of free will, but nature is undeniable regardless of prayers and the begging of forgiveness. I am who I am, impure yet righteous.

A satire on pregnancy

By Sadie Kaye / @sadie_artist (insta)

Readers of Transmuted will not need to be told about the Cass Review, how its methodology has excluded any real trans voice, how it treats being 'trans' as an illness to be 'cured', how it applies certain 'standards of proof' to some treatments but not others, and how the new Labour government plans to continue the ban of puberty-blocker treatment for trans youth. This piece was written to explore how the same methodology might be seen in another medical circumstance.

Dear sir,

You have asked me to address the problems of the condition known as 'pregnancy', why it continues to afflict so many people despite modern medical advances, and to review appropriate care for people that present with this mysterious condition.

Every year a significant number of people present with this condition. The numbers fluctuate considerably. For example, there was a significant epidemic of this disease in the early 1960s, sometimes referred to as the baby-boom. No one really understands why. Another oddity is that the individuals presenting with the condition are predominantly female, though the number of males with the condition has been increasing slightly in recent years. The condition itself is characterised by a swelling of the abdomen, severe mood-swings, and cravings for unusual foods. Towards the end of the incubation period, considerable pain is suffered and there is sometimes a substantial danger to life.

In my investigations into the issue, all submissions received were accepted at face value without questions. But you should be aware that, to ensure no bias in the data, I only accepted submissions from males. This is because it is a well-known symptom of pregnancy (even in its early undiagnosed stages) that it affects the minds of sufferers, and I did not want to accidentally skew the data with submissions from females who may be sufferers.

The submissions I considered were from medical experts in the field. I have divided the recommended treatments into two broad categories, which I have called 'normal' and 'crazy'.

The 'normal' treatment is described by the reasonable understanding that this pathological condition is serious, and is most likely caused by a delusion on the part of the sufferer. As a consequence the best course of action is to do nothing, let the disease take its course and hope the patient recovers and returns to normality. This usually takes a few months. Some practitioners recommend various procedures to encourage a speedy recovery. Of these, the surgical procedure known as 'D and C' seems particularly effective. The advocates of the 'normal' treatments typically do not suggest any medications, such as pain-killers.

The 'crazy' range of options that are endorsed by the other group of so-called experts do include pain-killers and other medicines to reduce the suffering of the patient. Surprisingly, one such treatment involves the use of nitrous oxide, a well-known recreational drug. Even more surprisingly, advocates of this approach recommend the patient self-administer the drug without limit on dosage. There is no academic study I am aware of that addresses the obvious problem of possible long term effects of this chemical in such patients. Other treatments include something called 'waterbirth' for which there is no scientific reason to believe this will have any significant effect, and until studies are carried out this is clearly a waste of money and could involve a possible danger of drowning. One individual consulted said that pregnancy is not a pathology at all, but a normal aspect of life. Obviously, since he was in a minority of one from a sample of several hundred I may safely disregard this unscientific opinion, but I record it here so that you understand how militant these 'crazy' experts can be.

My conclusions therefore are as follows. The 'normal' treatment has been used for several hundred years and needs no medical study to prove its effectiveness. The 'crazy' treatment has several significant problems that have not yet been addressed. In particular the use of recreational drugs is highly problematic; also, I was unable to find any satisfactory double-blind study on waterbirths. If this treatment is to be adopted it is essential that trials are performed in which neither the patient nor the medical practitioner is aware of whether or not a waterbirth is being used or not.

The health service's main priority should continue to be to understand the causes of this condition, and how epidemics arise, and not concern itself with the patients themselves, for whom the normal treatment of doing nothing is perfectly adequate.

Yours faithfully,
Tenzing Crass (Mr)

Butch-to-Butch

By Elijah Tiger / @elijahtiger (insta)

Will you take a moment with me?

Butch-to-Butch?

I worry that us Butches do not take care of our bodies enough. Are we crying enough, are we throwing our sorrow, pain, grief back into the wind enough? Are we feeling elation within our own bodies and image enough? Are we allowing ourselves to be with ourselves enough? We do not need to carry heavy feelings like pillars of rot.

And I work and I work all day and night

I wonder if I'm ever gonna get it right

I push and I push to get ahead

I know I gotta make my daily bread

I know I don't have time to lose

I wonder if I really have time to choose

I barely have time to shed a tear

I hardly have time to shake the fear (La Vita - Beverly Glenn-Copeland Lyrics)

Whilst reading Stone Butch Blues, an aspect that stuck with me the most was: the notion of being 'Stone'. What stuck with me is this shared fear of joy escaping us, which Leslie spoke on. For me, for a lot of my life, I've felt a fear of sitting in joy. That this wasn't what someone like myself was supposed to feel for too long. Long periods of joy wasn't something that was meant to become permanent - a home - for me. This was always at odds with the lessons my mother taught me - to enjoy your life, no matter what is thrown your way. But, I can't deny, it was always, and still sometimes is, so much easier to stay in the fear. To stay in the 'Stone'. To stay in this paralysis, which temporarily saves us from feeling it all.

There is a weight we might feel, as Butches, to balance it all. To be authentically ourselves, protecting the masculine that is important to us, sometimes afraid of what the vulnerability or perhaps perceived weakness might mean to the rest of the world, when we've fought so long and hard to get it right. However, vulnerability is the key to our joy, to our purest forms of expression. To deny ourselves, for fear of weakness, for fear of making a mistake, for fear of being taken for a fool - is to deny our greatest parts of ourselves.

I get it. I've fought long and hard enough to find this Butch within me and alight its world on fire, so that the world would see my beautiful masculinity. Sometimes I am too defiant for my own good. Too tough. This Butch can turn to Stone too often.

This leads me to want to know, to have to ask, my fellow Butch, how do you melt your Stone?

There are so many ways, aren't there? So many ways to soften and melt back into our feelings and our love, and allow vulnerability. I would like to share some of my own, and I would love for another Butch to hear me out. Deeply. I need another Butch to hear me out, deeply. I need another Butch, sometimes, to just hold me. I know you do too. I want to share a memory with you.

My mother grew up working-class, carrying a genetic physical Irish strength in her body. She has always moved her body and proved her strength. She didn't talk so much about her own feelings, but she is the softest woman in the world, who has a heart that burns away for all. Her feelings went into her statuesque body. I grew up watching her in the living room, with a baby on her, using strapped tins of tomatoes as weights in both hands, as she lunged across the room, back and forth for hours. She would do headstands against the wall whilst watching tv, stretching her legs whilst reading the tv guide. My mother was supposed to be a gymnast, yet she injured her wrist whilst young. Gymnastics and dance were the way my mother's strength melted into her beauty and her vulnerability; her pain and her joy.

Fast forward, a somewhat odd daughter/son, in her eyes, grew up - me. Music I got from my father, movement I got from my mother. I am a dancer. To dance is the only language I can speak fluently - and I'm a published writer and poet. Ha. It is the way I open up my body again, the way I can see my mother's body replicated within mine. My guide home.

The only way I can allow myself and the world to look at my vulnerability and I do not feel afraid. I look the audience in the eye and want them to see and feel it all. More importantly, I can face myself and feel good about all the feelings I have. And trust me, I have a lot. I am so soft really, and I love this about me. At the soft belly of what is me, is where you will find my joy, laughter. In moments of movement, it feels that joy will last forever for me, and it is my birthright. Through this, I discover over and over again: I am charming, soulful, cheeky, hopeful, sweet and silly.

My mother taught me the most fundamental lesson a Butch could need to know. To keep moving, in whatever capacity I can, through life; to keep accepting that joy could be a possibility at any corner I turn. That the only permanence I should avoid, is to stop, to be defeated, to give-in, and even to become stagnant within my Stone.

So, do something with me. Even just for 30 seconds. Put on 'La Vita' by Beverly Glenn-Copeland - a trans masculine elder who guides me daily. Find a mirror, look yourself in the eyes, then open your arms wide to the rhythm, bring them forward, look at your shoulders, your biceps, your chest, to your stomach; run your hands across yourself with care. Listen deeply to the words. Wiggle your fingers, your toes; roll your neck around, spin your body, find a new energy, be free. Think about someone who knows you, the whole you, it may be someone like your mother. For me, it is. Let their image of love wash over you, and if you can, let out a cathartic release. Let go. Go on, give yourself a smile/wink in the mirror whilst perhaps a few tears wet your cheeks, champ. You are beautiful, your Butch body is gorgeous; it deserves worship too.

Trans Lives in Early Film

By Edison Hipkin

The history of transgender film begins before the introduction of the term transgender in 1965, it begins before the prefix trans- is first used to describe gender variance in 1910, in fact it begins even before film started to take shape in the 1890s. To understand the early history of transgressive gender expression in film, we must first look to theatre.

Theatre has a long recorded history of cross-casting men in female roles and women in male roles. These roles are referred to in theatre as travesti, a term I will also use to refer to film performances. It differs from cross-dressing in film because cross-dressing is the act of a person who typically dresses in the clothes of one sex dressing in the opposite clothes for a limited time, travesti is for the entire length of the piece. Male to female travesti in theatre at end of the 19th century and the beginning of early film is often treated as joke, as a comedic role, much like pantomime dames still seen in British theatre, but at this time female to male travesti in theatre is beginning to become part of the dramatic mainstream, with popular actors like the American Maude Adams (made famous for playing male roles in L'Aiglon and Peter Pan and who is regarded by contemporary theorists as a queer woman) and the French Sarah Bernhardt (who originated the title male role in L'Aiglon and cemented her fame in both France and the United States playing Hamlet.)

While most 1900s theatrical stars dismissed film as a passing fad, Sarah Bernhardt wholeheartedly embraced the new medium. The earliest cinematic adaptation of Hamlet is in fact a scene performed by Bernhardt that premiered in 1900 as one of the central attractions of the 1900 Paris Exposition. The audience would be attracted to such a film by the performance of an esteemed actor like Bernhardt performing an intellectual and high culture play like Shakespeare, the fact that Bernhardt was playing a man was not noteworthy, especially compared to the high culture world of Shakespeare coming from a medium already associated with mass culture. While Sarah Bernhardt went on to play numerous other male roles in theatre, Hamlet is the only filmed record of this era of transgressive gender in media.

Similarly inspired by theatrical traditions, several films of the 1910s inspired by Italian commedia dell'arte and operatic traditions of cross-dressing and travesti. Renowned composer Gioachino Rossini wrote the opera Tancredi in 1813, the title character or Tancredi, an exiled male soldier hopelessly in love with a young noblewoman, was written to be sung by contralto voice type, so while an explicitly male character has been played by female opera singers since it's premiere. A hundred years later, Pierrot the Prodigal was released to wide commercial success. Pierrot the Prodigal, while a comedy about the stock pantomime character is similar to Tancredi as an explicitly male character that is in this inception played by Italian heartthrob and starlet Francesca Bertini.

Arguably the most famous cross-dresser of all time, Joan of Arc had fascinated and inspired artists since their death in 1431. By 1928, the year of the release of Carl Theodor Dreyer's The Passion of Joan of Arc, eight cinematic portrayals had already been made across France, America and the US. The Passion of Joan of Arc is set apart by its commitment to historical accuracy rather than a commitment to narrative storytelling, basing itself on historical transcripts of the trial of Joan of Arc. According to these transcripts taken at the time, Joan of Arc was tried and executed for cross-dressing and the heresy it was

supposedly evidence of. ("For nothing in the world will I swear not to [...] put on a man's dress.") Regardless of this, most artistic and cultural depictions of Joan of Arc present her as intrinsically feminine as the "Maid of Orléans", as exemplified in the American epic Joan the Woman, released just over a decade before The Passion of Joan Arc. Comparably this American Joan has shoulder length curled hair cut in a feminine bob style, and wears a skirt to battle. In The Passion of Joan of Arc, Dreyer's direction and the lauded performance of Renée Jeanne Falconetti in the lead role, instead choose to amplify Joan's masculinity, showing her with the close cropped hair and breeches not only typical for soldiers of the time but signifying masculinity to audiences in 1928. In 1936, only eight years after the release of the film, Joan of Arc was first discussed through a queer perspective in a biography by Vita Sackville-West. More recent queer and gender non conforming representations of Joan of Arc are featured in Leslie Feinberg's Transgender Warriors and Charlie Josephine's I, Joan. Dreyer's film clearly presents and discusses Joan as a trans-masculine character, while coming to no explicit conclusion on her identity, making it clear that Joan was an AFAB person who chose to dress is male clothing and was punished for it.

A year later in 1929, the G. W. Pabst directed Pandora's Box was released, the character of Countess Geschwitz in the film is often acknowledged to be the first explicitly lesbian character in cinema history. Unlike other early lesbian and sapphic characters, Geschwitz is characterised by her gender variance, she wears men's clothes, partakes in male activities like smoking and fulfils a male role in her attraction to women. Even outside of her sexual attraction she is a masculine character and could be defined as a butch lesbian character. On the other hand, Lulu, the protagonist of the film is a deeply androgynous and fluid character, with several clear female and male characteristics, not only in her way of dress but her outward expression. Her gender expression appears to depend on what helps her achieve her perceived "deviant" ambitions. Wedekind, the original creator of the character noted that "Lulu is not a real character, but the personification of primitive sexuality."

A pattern emerges amongst female bodied actors portraying male characters, and that is that it only occurs once in their career. Francesca Bertini only played a male character once in Pierrot the Prodigal (1914) Betty Bronson only played a male character in Peter Pan (1924) and even Sarah Bernhardt, acclaimed for playing multiple male roles on stage only transgressed gender once on the silver screen in Hamlet (1900). But to every rule there is an exception, and when discussing travesti and cross-dressing cinema and transmasculine characters, one name comes up again and again, and that is the Danish actor Asta Nielsen.

After making a single film in Denmark Asta Nielsen became an overnight European phenomenon, within a year she had moved to Berlin where she had been offered a contract and a studio exclusively for the making of her films. Her popularity in German silent cinema is credited to unique "boyish" appearance and portrayal of overtly sexual women, but Nielsen did not just play boyish or masculine women, she played male or transmasculine. First in Youth and Madness (1913) as Jesta, a playful young person who in an attempt to help their fiancés financial struggles spends most of the film dressed up as a man, engaging in male behaviour and even seducing a woman. Similarly in Zapata's Gang (1914) Nielsen plays an actress who ends up dressed as a man for the majority of the film, getting up to hijinks and seducing a young woman who appears not to care when in the finale they are revealed to be female. While both these protagonists begin and end the film as women, they spend the vast majority of the film presenting and living life as men. In 1916's The ABCs of Love, Nielsen again dons male garb, this time as a young romantic who, disappointed in her fiancés lack of

manliness, dresses as a man to teach her effeminate husband how to truly live life as a man. Out of the three "cross-dressing" films made by Nielsen, The ABCs of Love can most clearly be recognised as a transgender film about an AFAB person exploring and experimenting with what it means to become a man.

While these previously mentioned films are light-hearted, Nielen's final male role (and one of her most well-known) is a drama. The very same drama Sarah Bernhardt had played twenty years earlier. In 1921 Asta Nielsen played Hamlet, as a silent film, the exposition is explained via intertitles explaining to us that this Prince Hamlet, while assigned female at birth, has been raised and lives as a man in order to secure the line of succession to the mediaeval Danish throne. Here Nielsen plays a man who has been raised as such, who has been educated as stuff and who chooses to live his life as such even though he is still anatomically female (as revealed in the finale of the film). In Germany in 1921 we are presented with an empathetic explicitly trans-masculine character struggling through their life and their gender identity (in this interpretation of Hamlet one of the prince's key crises is his fight between his masculine and feminine natures) in a way even modern audiences are starved of.

Inspired by these continental films and earlier theatrical traditions, female masculinity first hit America in 1930 with the immigration of German film star and bisexual woman, Marlene Dietrich. In her first Hollywood film Morocco, Dietrich plays a cabaret performer who as part of her act performs as a male impersonator (drag king). While performing her act Dietrich's character flirts with and kisses a female audience member in one of the earliest sapphic kisses in mainstream film, but also in an early representation of a gender non conforming character. These representations of trans-masculine people passed through national borders and these lives and characters were openly presented to mass audiences in the era of silent films.

While these early films mentioned can easily be seen to have transgender or transsexual characters or themes inside of their narratives, it has to be noted that it was during this era of film that the first transsexual and gender-non-conforming people were first seen on screen. The film was Different From The Others, a 1919 feature film funded by the Institute of Sexual Science and co-written by Magnus Hirschfeld (the man credited with introducing the prefix of trans- in transvestite and transsexual.) In the film a successful homosexual artist is blackmailed because of his sexuality. The film is noted as one of the earliest explicit and empathetic portrayals of queer lives and characters. In a short scene, Hirschfeld appears as himself, leading a public lecture on sexual diversity where he shows images of transgender men and butch women as well as transgender women. Hirschfeld was keen to use this film to advocate for the rights of sexual minorities, specifically targeting German legislation that criminalised homosexual activity. The film was banned by a specifically created board of censors only a year after its release. While films with adult or queer content were routinely banned for youth consumption in the Weimar Republic, Different From The Others is one of the very few German-made films known to have been censored inside of Germany. Even now the film only exists in extracts and fragments.

The open portrayal of transgressive gender in European Expressionist cinema was allowed in mainstream film because of the liberal and progressive climate it was produced in. This era of the 1910s and 1920s was quickly overcome and overshadowed by the rise of fascism and dawning of war across Europe. European cinema fell into decline and Hollywood prospered with the introduction of sound film in 1927 and the development of colour film throughout the 1930s. Several of the films discussed are lost or only exist in fragments preserved by various film institutes leaving limited visual evidence behind of this interwar period of queer liberation on screen.

TERFism, Transphobia and the 2024 Paris Olympics

By J. S. Gupta

In 2023, I wrote a three part polemic for this publication entitled 'Are TERFs Fascists'. These articles were an analysis and critique of TERFist ideology.

'TERF', for those unfamiliar, is an acronym for 'Trans Exclusionary Radical Feminist'. It is a term used to describe a specific strain of transphobia that has appropriated feminism as a means to mask and legitimise their fascistic vitriol.

In this article I spent some time dissecting and refuting the arguments of the TERFs, spending a good chunk of the piece talking about the TERF's attempts to use pseudo-biological arguments in their rhetoric against trans people and trans existence.

In Part 2, I wrote:

> TERFs will strictly define what physical traits are to be considered 'masculine' and what traits are to be considered 'feminine'. This is in an attempt to 'prove' that trans women are not 'real women', as well an attempt to shame and humiliate trans women for not conforming to set physical standards. Broad shoulders, narrow hips, large jaws, facial hair, thinning hair - all physical traits that can, and are, possessed by cis women, but are traits that TERFs prescribe upon trans women in an effort to paint all trans women as the transphobic caricature of a 'man in a dress'. In effect, TERFs ultimately shame and alienate cis women who have supposedly 'masculine' physical traits of their own. Many cis women have been on the receiving end of transphobia, being purposefully misgendered or treated with contempt. There have even been instances of cis women being confronted in bathrooms as they have been 'clocked' as transgender. The TERFs are obsessed with trans women's ability to 'pass' as 'real women', insisting they don't 'pass' and will never 'pass' and claiming they can 'clock' a woman as transgender very easily. TERFs and other transphobes have made a sort of game out of this. In reality, this 'clocking' merely results in the harassment and oppression of all women.

Though these three articles combined were already quite long, I felt I did not go into as much depth as I wanted in exploring these issues, particularly in looking at non-visible physical traits that may be considered 'masculine'.

And earlier, in Part 1, I also wrote:

> However, most of the major organisations, their most prominent leaders and the women who typically attend TERFist meetings, are women of privilege, women of means. What is interesting when we begin to consider this about TERFs, is that both a woman's whiteness and her economic access to the means of production are directly related to conceptions of femaleness and femininity, their femininity often seen as the default mode of femininity or idealised femaleness. Working class women and non-white women (especially black women) are often demeaned by women of privilege as having more 'masculine' qualities.

This was something I originally began expanding upon while writing the original article but quickly realised such analysis would take up too much of the piece potentially distract from the central point I was trying make. However, due to recent events, I found myself thinking about these sections of that article and how I felt I needed to finally look a little deeper at both of these points.

The events (or rather event) in question is the transphobia that an Algerian boxer has been experiencing this year, during her time competing in the 2024 Olympic Games in Paris. And though it is transphobia that she is experiencing, the boxer, Imane Khelif, is not a trans woman but in fact a cisgender woman. After medical tests performed ahead of the World Boxing Championships in 2023, she was disqualified for having 'high testosterone' as well as XY Chromosomes. This is unusual, but not unheard of for cisgender women (i.e. women assigned female at birth). If the tests performed by the IBA[1] are in fact correct, Khelif may be considered intersex, which means that her biological sex exists outside of the rigidly defined sexes of 'male' and 'female' and the 'normal' levels of hormones and 'normal' chromosomes determined for each. Khelif herself has not identified as intersex, however,

---

1   International Boxing Association

and the IBA may not be fully trustworthy for various reasons[2]. Further the notion of 'normal' when it comes to biological sex is inherently flawed and, if you will allow me get a little radical, may be evidence that the binary sex paradigm is effectively incorrect. Sex, like gender, is more complex and more varied than the cisgenders have led us to believe.

The claims of high testosterone and XY Chromosomes followed Khelif through her whole time competing at the Games along with some extremely transphobic rhetoric. This became especially loud after she defeated an Italian boxer, Angela Carini, in 46 seconds, during the second round of the tournament for the Welterweight division. And when she went on to win the whole tournament, taking home the gold and winning Algeria its first gold medal in boxing, there was more outcry by the usual suspects.

The simple fact that Imane Khelif came from a country that did not recognise transgender people, yet was being defended by the Algerian Olympic Committee, did not seem to sway these people. Nor did the reality that the IBA's supposed testing was suspect. The transphobes of the world have a narrative they need to push, they have propaganda they want to spread and an ideology they want to impose on the world. Science, facts and logic have no space in the camp of the cisgenderist ideologues and extremists.

Transphobes want to push the agenda that trans people (and queer people in general) existing openly in society is harmful to society. And a key part of their propaganda is that trans existence is harmful to cisgender women. This propaganda has invaded the world of sport for quite some time, the apparent fear that a trans or queer person might participate in an international sporting competition and maybe even win. There's nothing rational about transphobia, it's purely emotive and not driven by genuine concern for athletes, certainly not the female athletes they ignore the majority of the time, but driven by a sheer hatred for all those people who do not conform to an arbitrarily defined conception of normativity.

But of course Imane Khelif isn't trans, but that doesn't matter to these people. They see a woman who doesn't fit their standards of 'femaleness' and so they targeted her with hate and harassment in one of the most disgusting smear

---

[2] https://www.bbc.co.uk/sport/boxing/68718463

campaigns in recent memory. Especially ghoulish are the TERFs that were involved with this, the female transphobes who claim their transphobia is some sort of feminism. The disparagement of a fellow cisgender woman for not fitting patriarchal standards of femininity is beyond hypocrisy and beyond parody. The fact that these people led an international hate campaign against this woman based on limited evidence of her apparent trans-ness, is demonstratable evidence for how deranged the members of TERF movement truly are. They saw someone who served neatly as 'evidence' that served their agenda, and they used Khelif to propagate bigotry, rather than celebrate a woman who had achieved something remarkable.

And there is a racial dimension here that cannot go overlooked. It seems that women of colour like Khelif, particularly women of African descent, tend to be subjected to the most scrutiny regarding their femininity. Women of colour, are often imbued with masculine traits by white imaginations, perceived as more aggressive and violent than white women. Outside of personality, the physical traits women of colour often have are not typically considered part of the hegemonic ideal of femininity – fair skin, long silky hair, low body hair, small build and stature and so on. And so much of this can intersect with class where wealthier women of colour can afford treatments to make themselves appear less 'ethnic' and more in-line with the ideals of femaleness. Hegemonic beauty standards for women are typically defined by the white majority in the metropole/imperial core, creating an ideal that women outside of a narrow array can struggle to reach. And this is something that is rooted in colonialism, in the racial hierarchy upheld at the height of European colonialism. Male race scientists were concocted these constructions of ideal human existence to justify the violence being imposed up on the colonised world. And it has to be said, the fact that the initial outrage over Khelif was due to her making a white woman (Carini) cry cannot be considered incidental.

The disparagement and cruel remarks faced by Khelif has not been too different to those received by many women of colour such as those who grow up in white majority countries. And the treatment of Khelif is not new to sports either. Another African Olympic gold medallist, Caster Semenya, faced scrutiny and was forced to undergo 'sex testing' for due to people believing she was 'too male' to be competing in women's athletics. Semenya is a long-distance runner from South Africa who was disqualified from competing after it was discovered that her testosterone was naturally too high compared to that of a 'normal woman'. Semenya isn't alone either. Two female Namibian athletes were ruled ineligible to compete at the Tokyo Games for their high testosterone. To be clear, these are all cisgender women, assigned female at birth, with hormone levels that naturally differ from the 'average woman' (or at least whatever that's been ideologically determined to be). They are not 'doping', they are merely divergent from what has been considered 'normalcy'. But that is something that is true for so many athletes competing at a high-level at any international competition. But transphobia (in combination with Misogynoir) has determined this little genetic divergence to be unacceptable.

The Olympics, for all their many, many faults, are a celebration of human variation. Of the divergence of our species. Watching this year I saw so many men and women of varying body types, bodies made to perform at this high level; bodies made to break world records and win medals. Few women at the Olympics fit the idealised hegemonic standards for female beauty. They have honed their bodies to serve the sports they compete in, not to serve the male gaze. The fact Olympics showcases women who exist outside of the supermodel aesthetic, making great athletic achievements should be something celebrated by feminists. Instead these Games were marred by a hate campaign against a woman who did not fit into the narrow box of idealised femininity.

This was misogyny, plain and simple. This was hatred against a woman for not living up to patriarchal standards of femaleness. And transphobia has made this behaviour so much worse. The panic about the 'transgenders among us' has led to this moment, the beginning of the cannibalisation of other cisgender women by TERFs, supported by male transphobes.

The term 'transvestigating' has cropped up online in recent years, a term to describe this phenomenon of the cisgenders trying to figure out who's trans. These terminally online types, partaking in the most amateurish detective work, based only on pseudo-scientific conceptions of female anatomy. There is considerable crossover between this type of 'investigatory' work and the so-called 'body language exerts' that exist online. And it is resulting in accusations being made against cisgender women and even some cisgender men. These people have the attitude and outlook of the most unhinged conspiracy theorists. They've gone as far as 'transvestigating' each other, TERFs accusing other TERFs of being trans. Hopefully this results in them destroying themselves, though of course in the interim they will cause a lot of harm against innocent transgender and cisgender people with their hate and harassment.

The ideals of 'true femininity' and 'true masculinity' are considered ideals due to the reality that they are social constructions dreamt up by human imaginations. And like most ideals, they are not something that can be achieved. Human beings of all genders and sexes are naturally diverse and varied in body type, in their facial features, in their genetic and chemical composition. So many humans have made themselves miserable trying to conform to these arbitrarily determined constructs of sex and gender; trying to present themselves in a way that is "true femininity" or "true masculinity". It's why the trans movement, as well as the wider queer movement, has been so liberating for so many. It's freed people from the mental constrictions placed on them by a cisnormative society. People have been allowed to find happiness in being themselves. TERFs on the other hand are a truly miserable bunch. They're self-hating women with an extreme, internalised misogyny that they inflict on innocent women. They'll never find liberation within their hive of fascistic hatred. They will only continue to make themselves and each other miserable.

Imane Khelif is not trans but she has been excluded from cis-femininity by transphobes. This is a form of alienation the queer community knows all to well. She is one of us, another individual that has been mistreated for not conforming to gender normativity. We must extend solidarity to her and other people like her. Bigots have attempted to belittle and obscure Khelif's athletic success and achievement. Her medals are well deserved and people should celebrate her and her accomplishments. Khelif has also filed a criminal complaint against the ring leaders of the transphobic harassment against her, including several notable celebrities. Her success in these proceedings will set a valuable precedent and hopefully make transphobes think twice before they open their mouths in the future.

Film Review: Trailblazers (2024, Sobia Bushra)

By Dorian Rose / @generefuccere (insta)

In a dimly-lit room, a DJ prepares for their set. Over at the bar, the bartender prepares a customer's drink, placing a red-white straw in an icey half-pint glass. We don't see anyone's faces just yet – just their expressive clothing, the movement of hands, an exquisite spectrum of kicks. A quiet excitement hangs in the air before the ballroom performance begins – cheering, chanting builds as someone introduces us to the set on a microphone.

Bristol, The Fruitea Ball

Trailblazers is a documentary about Asian Purrrsuasion, the Welsh Ballroom community, and being a queer South Asian in Wales today.

Sobia Bushra's documentary is a monumental film following the co-founders of Asian Purrrsuasion (Alia Milan, Muz 'Supreme' Razman, and Aiman Rahim) – who use this space to simply speak about themselves. Of finding liberation from life's difficulties in community, performance, and self-expression.

Through individual interviews and visually-stunning moments with the trio, we follow a story - their stories, of ballroom and Asian Purrrsuasion. We're thrust into fast-paced and upbeat moments, dipped into the slow and harsh realities of difference, then communally rejoicing in the presence of freedom, community, and love.

The film, and the work of Asian Purrrsuasian, highlights the issues faced by queerness, loneliness, and difference in a normative society. We learn about modern-day ballroom, the multitudes of performance, and how Alia, Aiman, and Muz work today to inspire, fight, and trailblaze for South Asian queer communities. Though we might have to leave our childhood caregivers and family behind, despite our difficulties to

Alia and Muz busting out moves in perhaps the greatest documentary scene to date.

connect with our generational cultures we can find them again in each other.

All while enjoying some energetic dancing, graceful couture, and dynamic cinematography.

Alia Ramna and Muz Razman are the first we're introduced to. While Aiman enters around halfway through the short film, they have perhaps the most quotable things to say…

Aiman Rahim performing for a sold-out crowd, Kahani Raat (Night) at the Wales Millenium Centre in Cardiff

"I want South Asians, especially queer South Asians, to know that they don't need to run away from their culture in order to be queer."

Muz also quotes Beyonce: "if they're not giving you a space on stage, you build your own."

Occupy space - says Trailblazers - and fill it with friends, new family, and celebration. That, and much more.

We're shown those personal moments where reality hits, when you get back to your someone-else's home, when bills have to be paid and moths flutter out of your wallet, when we have to sit in lonely silence with our mountain of problems. But Bushra picks us back up, puts us into the joys and nerves of performance, and reminds us that we're not alone.

These moments pull at those infamous heartstrings, not simply because the all-too-common realities of financial difficulties are wantonly unjust, but because we as the audience are allowed to glide from one moment to the next – but Muz, our guide through this particular melancholy, cannot jump-cut to the crowd of a club (in full glam, dressed to the gods) as we do in this film. None of us can.

But what Bushra does in these moments is incredibly therapeutic. We're shown that, despite the moments of suffering, we can still find our joy over the horizon.

At the same time, Bushra shows us a real problem: financial insecurity, houselessness, alienation, and a lack of community among queer folks

By Dorian Rose

Muz cracks a lot of jokes to keep us on our toes.

Backstage at Kahani Raat (Night). (Left to right: Lady Bushra, Alia Ramna, Aiman Rahim, Muz 'Supreme' Razman).

– among QTIPOC, people without safety, or that familial connection that can be so vital in times of financial difficulty.

But all of this is just one aspect of Trailblazers, and of Asian Purrrsuasion's work. This film gives us the ability to self-reflect on our communities, what we can do to support each other. And perhaps most importantly, a chance to feel emotions that you might have pushed down in order to survive.

Trailblazers is a work that will inspire you to keep fighting. And, uniquely, shows us how three living legends fight for us today.

Trailblazers premiered at Chapter Arts Centre in Cardiff, Wales, on the 29th of September at 7.30PM.

Directed by Sobia Bushra

Produced by Ronan Williams

Film Review: Orlando, My Political Biography (2023, Paul B. Preciado)

By Rebys J Hynes & Dorian Rose / @rebysjhynes, @generefuccere (IG)

Rebys

I write this on a cloudy Saturday morning before my first Pride. I have been living as an out-non-binary person for four years, wrote for queer zines, lived a queer life, and have yet to do a Pride. At a time when Tesco keeps its flags up two weeks after June ends just to avoid accusations of Rainbow Capitalism, and our fresh new government still can't commit to banning conversion therapy, and supporters of genocide try to pinkwash by pretending to support our liberation, finding pride in Pride is a difficult thing to do. But today we march as a protest, like every Pride before us. I tell you this because the film we're about to discuss is all about the context of living as a trans person today. To situate a discussion of the fictional in our-every day lives.

My name is Rebys J. Hynes and in this review, I'll be Virginia Woolf's Orlando.

Orlando, My Political Biography (2023, Paul B. Preciado) is a French documentary film that has just finished its limited run in UK cinemas. Through interviews with twenty-six trans people and one dog, Preciado transformatively retells Virginia Woolf's landmark queer text, to explore trans lives and bodies, cisgenderism, pharmaceutical liberation amongst many other issues that affect trans and gender-non-conforming people.

21 different actors play Orlando – each introducing themselves as 'Virginia Woolf's Orlando' – defying any sort of stable categorisation for the literary figure. It is a film that is non-binary on every level.

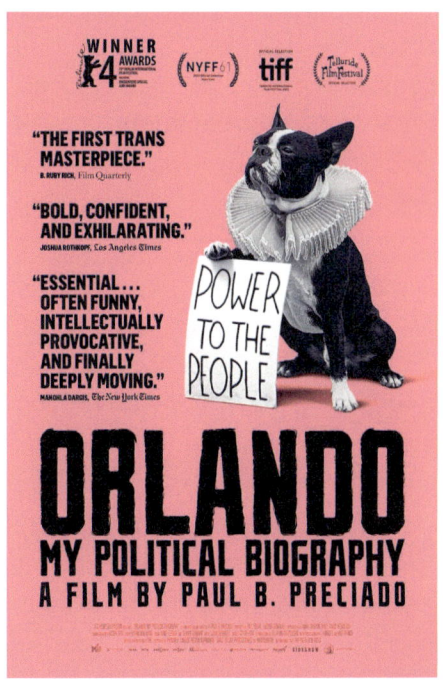

It is a documentary and it is fiction and it is neither. People play themselves and the characters of Orlando and both. It is a retelling and it is an essay and a critique and, at times, nothing even remotely like any of those things. It is a stunning work of cinema unlike anything I've ever seen before. It is a film that is fundamentally trans. I hope, truly and deeply, that is the harbinger of a beautiful trans cinema to come.

I first saw the film at the Edinburgh International Film Festival last year, determined to make it to the morning screening as I thought it would be my only chance to ever see the film. Getting the opportunity to see it again this week has been lovely. The first time, I saw it with my Mum and it prompted a lovely discussion in Edinburgh Street Food about my own trans journey. The second time, I saw it with queer friends. Both times, seeing it alongside the broader audience was a transformational experience. The audiences were flooded with trans and gender non-conforming people. The act of putting on these films changed these spaces – I love the indie cinema circuit, but it's rare I will see more than one or two trans people at any screening at a time. To sit with an audience majority comprised of trans people is a privilege and an experience. Queer curation and queer programming is one of the first steps in creating queer spaces.

I have so many things about the film that I want to ask you, Dorian. But let's start nice and simple:

What did you think of the film?

Dorian

First of all – hello, my name is Dorian and in this review I'll be Virginia Woolf's Orlando. Gotta keep up with the vibes.

I should preface this by saying that your experience in viewing Orlando: My Political Biography shows a stark contrast to my own – sat at home eating biscuits, trying to intellectualise every scene. I ended up stewing in a broth of my own tears, cursing this cruel world for its views on gender.

Despite (or maybe due to) my attempts to critically view the film instead of simply watching, I felt like my very soul was being spread on an incredibly intellectual slice of filmic toast. As Orlando kept playing I slowly melted into its metaphors and stories, resulting in a soggy end to digest this imaginary trans liberation, and to sip on life's woes.

Orlando is as artsy a film as you can get, by no means a simple watch. In spite of this, it is easy to become engrossed in its storytelling, in its world and characters.

While Orlando guides you through many complicated depictions of trans life, history, and politics – it does so unapologetically, with a peaceful pride, gracefully passing through each story like chapters of a book.

We're taught at once about Virginia Woolf's Orlando, her life; trans life, politics, and history; but also about ourselves. Every moment of the film is a point to self-reflect upon (making for a very good catalyst to any mid-life crisis you're thinking about starting).

Weeping my eyes out during the credits, I had my own realisation to the incredible ways that transphobia has affected my view of the world. I wanted to exist in this film, not only to celebrate my queerness, but to enjoy it like I enjoy air. To be free to express myself through the liberation and love of all those around me. That is what Orlando is about: the abundance of queerness, and the should-be right for it to flow with the wind. Well, that and everything else.

There is one scene in Orlando depicting (quite accurately) the experience of pathologisation that many trans folks have to go through.

Frederic Pierrot looks into the camera, announcing to the audience that he 'will be Dr Queen, a psychiatrist'. He is here to represent the Queen and imperial power within Woolf's Orlando and Preciado's Orlando: My Political Biography. As the scene opens, in his practice are multiple trans patients with whom we get to see glimpses of in Dr Queen's office and his waiting room. We sit in a session with one such patient, Orlando (played by Liz Kristin). Dr Queen pathologises their 'transness', at one point emphasising genitalia. Orlando responds by expressing fondness with their 'feminine penis'. Queen dictates that there is 'biological reality' and 'fantasy', questioning Orlando on the gender of their sperm. Orlando responds with brilliant confidence, expressing the biological reality that neither genitals nor body fluids have a gender, and that to believe they do is "an invention of modernity."

To watch this scene is at once

horrifying (harkening back to our own experiences) and liberating. Seeing Orlando have the confidence to express themselves with knowledge abundant within trans communities felt like free therapy. Of course, many trans people avoid arguing with doctors about the realities of gender: fearing the refusal of treatment or complications therein.

All the while this scene signifies a modern take on Woolf's story - where in the book, Orlando's gender is put towards medical debate. What a moment to behold!

And this leads me to ask, what do you think about this 'fuck the cistem' rhetoric in Preciado's Orlando?

Rebys

I love the multitude of ways in which this film says 'fuck the cistem', in railing against the oppressive and failing medical system, in reclaiming joy in our bodies and our transitions and our experiences. My favourite thing about this movie is all the queer space it creates. Even in Dr. Queen's waiting room - a liminal space in which we must wait before being subject to invasive and patronising interrogation – the trans characters, the Orlandos, forge a queer space.

One in which the cistem is mocked and trans people can sit and openly discuss their struggles and their issues. In which they administer HRT to each other because why wait around for the system to fail you? All of this whilst they erupt into the campy yet revolutionary bop that is that the 'Pharmacoliberation' song. That one line, 'You might be synthetic but not apologetic / You're not the doctor's bitch' was on loop in my head for days after watching.

And it's not just in the office are queer spaces built and relished. The woods, a film set, a courthouse, in this film all become places where we can live beyond the cisgender gaze. Where our bodies are not subject to their eyes and our rights are not theirs to take away. It's perhaps fair to say that this film less says 'fuck the cistem' and more 'long live trans liberation'. It criticises the powers that try to control us, but the film's true revolution is in the beautiful freedom of trans life. That's how I felt watching this film – beautiful. In a world of trans liberation, we are thriving and we are beautiful.

That closing scene is so striking as a result. I would love to hear your thoughts on it! The film ends in a post-revolution world, where the cistem has fell and trans liberation has been achieved. It dreams that that future is only a few years away, which is perhaps a little optimistic. But it is the dream that is wonderful. The film luxuriates in that final scene – it goes on for so long, we hear everyone get the liberation they deserve – and in the slow pace, the film stresses each individual life that will be elevated by liberation.

I find it interesting that you call it artsy, because I've come to think of it as being almost the exact opposite. Don't get me wrong, the premise of a documentary-fiction-adaptation-not-adaptation sounds pretty damn artsy, and I did literally see it first at a film festival so that's another notch in the artsy column, but I have come to think of this film as super low art and I love it. It's a bit shoddy at times. Cheap and camply so, and there are moments where it almost felt like I was watching a high-budget student film (complementary). There are risque jokes and queer jokes galore – what do you expect from a film that includes in its cast the role of 'Goddess of Gender Fucking'. It really does seem artsy at first, with its allusions to a classical literary text and its deconstructive approach. But get past that, and you have a really accessible, camp, joyous picture.

It's as I write this now that I realise what Orlando reminds me of. It's not a piece that is high-art or low, its not documentary nor fiction. It is a zine. A filmic zine. It has that DIY feel, of a bunch of people coming together and sharing their experiences, creating art together that exists on the periphery of the system. It is how stitched together it feels, whilst still having a cohesive vision across its entirety. It is subversive and even though it has featured at film festivals and had a limited release, it really feels underground. I love what you said about every moment of this film being a point to self-reflect upon – it perfectly summarises how this film is brimming with ideas and catalysts for understanding of the self and of society. It is a manifesto, it is a thoroughly non-binary text, and it is closest I've ever known to seeing a zine on the big screen.

I have two questions for you? First, have you read Orlando? I haven't, and I would be fascinated to discuss the difference in experiences between those who have read the base text and those who have not?

And second, I am intrigued by this film's lack of discussion of pronouns. It talks extensively about surgeries and experiences and legal recognition, yet there is little to no mention of pronouns – a facet of trans identity that tends to dominate modern discourse.

What do you think of this absence of pronouns?

Dorian

You've caught me red-handed: I haven't read Woolf's Orlando either! The intermittent explanations of Woolf's novel were very welcome in my noggin, and rendered the watching process something like the greatest lecture I've ever had. But this makes the discussion of difference futile indeed.

I do find it a very 'non-binary' film, for lack of a better term. There is simply no reason to discuss pronouns in general throughout the film, so it simply doesn't. It is one aspect that makes the film distinctly trans for trans: there is a distinct lack of pandering towards a cisgender audience. It doesn't try to explain any aspect of trans existence, whatever explanation is given is purely a side effect.

There's a whole bunch of trans people out here with a whole bunch of different lived experiences. The ways in which we tend to explain our 'transness', all intrinsically unique to each person, are through the cisgender gaze – or should I say, the cisgender mouth. Our pronouns are one such effect of the imposition of their tongue into our throats (sorry for that picture). And there is something powerful about language: it is emotional, it is full of context, and it holds power. In removing something as simple as pronouns from our art, we are able to remove the power that cisnormativity holds upon us, even within us. Of course, this doesn't work in cisnormative spaces (because the pronoun is unspoken), but within transnormative spaces we find freedom – just from this small act.

It is art such as this that can revolutionise our ways of thinking, our lives, and our communities. Resistance is not just existence – resistance is existence when we also share it with others: occupying normative spaces, creating art, having conversations, and finding confidence within ourselves and ourselves-with-others. An inconceivable amount of trans folks find themselves lonely, sometimes alone too – and art like Preciado's Orlando can help to combat that.

Rebys

I find it so wonderful that neither of us have read Orlando and yet we are still overflowing with love for this film! To me, that shows that

1.) this film does a great job of guiding you through the plot of the novel and

2) it's not really about Viriginia Woolf's Orlando at all.

It is about the stories that have come before us that we see ourselves in. Nearly every trans person has a weird, messy pop culture piece they can point to and say 'there, that is where I saw myself'. I have a list as long as this review. My Political Biography is less about the text of Orlando, and more about seeing your 'biography' in somebody else's story.

I adore this idea of a T4T cinema! I have seen three films with trans content in the cinema over the last month: Orlando, Crossing and I Saw the TV Glow. Crossing has some good moments and it is great to see trans sex workers' lives depicted on screen, but with its focus on cis characters and cis guilt it struggled to feel like the sort of trans cinema I wanted. I mention this because the audience for this film was predominantly comprised of cis people (as far as I am aware – of course I am cis passing 50% of the time). Whereas when I saw both Orlando and I Saw the TV Glow, both screenings were overflowing with trans/ visibly queer people. These are films made by trans people, for trans people. With these films screening across the UK, bringing trans audiences to see trans films, we are starting to see a model for a T4T cinema and that is just beyond beautiful.

Before we wrap up, I want to really highlight what you just said. Resistance is existence when we also share it with others. I have read this sentence over and over again because I find it just beautiful. This world, as a trans person, right now, not the best. But I share this world with my trans siblings and my queer family. This film, this conversation, our lives, we share and we exist and we resist. T4T cinema can really help us usher in a T4T world.

I love this film not only because it is a wonderful piece of cinema, but also because it has inspired so much introspection and reflection and it has led to this conversation, which I have thoroughly enjoyed having with you.

Dorian

Thank you so much for sharing this space with me Rebys, for your kind and extensive commentary, and for anyone who has made it this far in reading!

As we move on, I hope that we can find more ways to bring this type of cinema, of creativity, to more trans folks who need it most. I, for one, find it incredibly difficult to access the various events and spaces where I can revel in all our trans glory.

If you're like me and have little ability to travel, I'd like to point out the esteemed poets Jaime Lock, George Parker, JP Seabright, and their recently released pamphlet Not Your Orlando – which you can buy online for delivery! Despite being completely removed from the world of Orlando: My Political Biography (in fact George said they'd never even heard of the film), the film and the pamphlet go almost hand in hand – they should be available at all viewings!

It is exactly these moments where we discuss our joys, our experiences and lows, that build ourselves in stronger community. We find ourselves in each other, as they so eloquently put it:

*"it's okay to be like this
there's nothing broken
nothing to fix
this is who we are
this is how it is"*

-Cwtch Butch, *Not Your Orlando* by Jaime Lock, George Parker, JP Seabright (2024, Punk Dust Poetry, page 39).

Love and solidarity,

Rebys J. Hynes & Dorian Rose xo

Call for Submissions

Interested in submitting? Here's some info:

As Transmuted is a journal for transgender, gender non-normative, nonconforming, non-binary, non-gender, and so on: we ask for submissions only by people who identify with the subject matter of the journal (non-cis).

We are a transgender-oriented journal, so we ask for submissions related to gender: whether it's direct or indirectly related to issues with the cisgender norm, we don't mind.

We accept all kinds of work: digital art, photography, poetry, short stories, opinion pieces, essays, articles, reviews – anything else, submit it and we'll see if we can make it work!

If you're worried about spelling, grammar, style, titles – we're always available to talk about your worries, so hit us up! This is a place for emotion, connection, and ideas – whatever you create has a space, and we'd love to share your work or even just be a space for public ranting.

For written contributions, we tend to accept anything from a few lines or words to 4,000 words, depending on the genre of your work.

Any submission may be completely anonymous or authored to a pseudonym according to how you would prefer it. Send us an email from an anonymous account, and/or you can use a pesudonym for your work to be attributed to.

Send your submission to us by

Email: contactus@transmuted.co.uk or

Website form: www.transmuted.co.uk/submit

Please go to www.transmuted.co.uk/submit for more guidelines.

About Transmuted

What is Transmuted?

Transmuted is an independent trans organisation based in England (currently directed by two absolute eggs).

Our primary goal is to strengthen alternative voices within trans spaces; to amplify the voices that are repeatedly silenced by wider society. To support & celebrate the trans community, help build links, mutual understanding and solidarity between ourselves and the wider community.

Aims

1. Creating spaces and platforms for trans people of all backgrounds to share their work (especially internationally & online).

2. Establishing safe spaces to learn and be ourselves.

3. To inspire and support trans arts and culture in all mediums.

4. Making trans culture more accessible to trans and non-trans people.

5. Giving the proverbial microphone to trans people, allowing them to represent themselves.

6. Employing our abundant trans creativity to challenge transphobia as a collective.

One of our key projects is our journal, also called 'Transmuted', which we have been releasing quarterly - now annually.

The journal is one space we've created to platform trans artists and scholars, to elevate their voices and allow them to share their perspectives and experiences.

We also host a number of events each year, both in-person and virtually

These include workshops that allow for community education, knowledge-sharing and open discussion.

Please contact us via the email below if you'd like to:

Stock our products: stickers, posters, art prints, journals, and zines for your shop.

Use our products to fundraise for your group / organisation / gender affirming care / project / etc.

Hire our team for events, illustration, design, editing, and/or proofreading.

How to Support us

Despite being a very small organisation run by a very small but eager and committed team, our costs are substantial.

We would really appreciate any financial support we can get to 'keep the lights on' and to help us make this project bigger and reach as many people as possible.

The easiest way to support us is to subscribe to our journal or purchase stickers, prints and other things from our online shop.

The best way to support us is through direct donations. Please consider a monthly donation on our Patreon. Just a couple of pounds a month can help make a big difference in helping us promote trans voices. You can also provide a one time donation on PayPal.

Email: contactus@transmuted.co.uk.

Instagram, TikTok, and YouTube: @trans_muted

Facebook: Transmuted CIC

Down

1. (5, 5) Support networks of friends who take the place of unsupportive relatives.
4. The discomfort some trans individuals feel due to a mismatch between their body and assigned gender.
5. The act of being seen and acknowledged, often celebrated on March 31.
6. Living as one's true gender without disclosing one's 'transness'.
7. An historical colour associated with 2SLGBTQIA+ movements.
12. Words like 'he', 'xe', or 'they' that affirm a person's gender.
14. The act of reclaiming one's identity and autonomy.
15. A person fighting for equality, representation, and justice.
16. A celebration of 2SLGBTQIA+ identities and communities, held every June.

Across

2. A term often used in gender-affirming surgery discussions, referring to surgeries involving the lower body.
3. A word reclaimed by some 2SLGBTIQIA+ folks (with derogatory roots).
8. The 1969 uprising that is often marked a turning point in 2SLGBTQIA+ history.
9. A supportive person advocating for trans and 2SLGBTQIA+ rights.
10. A garment often worn by transmasculine individuals to flatten the chest.
11. Recognising overlapping systems of discrimination that affect all marginalised folks.
13. A way to describe the diversity and fluidity of gender.
17. The process of aligning one's presentation and identity with their gender.
18. Abbreviation for a medical process involving hormones for gender affirmation.
19. A gender identity that exists outside the traditional male and female categories.

To see the answers, go to www.transmuted.co.uk/issue-10-crossword-answers